On Censorship

The Speaker's Corner Books Series

Speaker's Corner Books is a series of book-length essays on important social, political, scientific, and cultural topics. Originally created in 2005, the series is inspired by Speakers' Corner in London's Hyde Park, a bastion of free speech and expression. The series is influenced by the legacy of Michel de Montaigne, who first raised the essay to an art form. The essence of the series is to promote life-long learning, introducing the public to interesting and important topics through short essays, while highlighting the voices of contributors who have something significant and important to share with the world.

"Between book banning and cancel culture, Americans are awash in confusing questions of censorship. In this fascinating essay, James LaRue proves a whip-smart, steady guide through the mire. LaRue, a staunch defender of the free exchange of ideas, exposes the hypocrisy of those who seek to muzzle others, using anecdotes from his long career as a respected librarian. He also provides common sense ways to combat censorship movements. Offering invaluable insight into the issue, this work is not only for librarians, but for anyone trying to make sense of our conflicted, overheated, and often-exasperating modern world."

—**Patti Thorn**, BlueInk Review

"An insightful and humorous look into the complex issues of censorship, Jamie LaRue's book is at times intellectually and emotionally challenging—like all of the best books should be."

—**R. Alan Brooks**, Comics Creator and Professor, Professor of Graphic Narrative, Regis University, www.ralanwrites.com

"Generous gifts of wisdom, encouragement, and practical guidance are packed into this brief exploration of a perennially challenging issue. Jamie LaRue is one of the heroes of American libraries' long history of service and growth in difficult times. He delivers his deeply considered, hopeful message, as always, with memorable wit and charm. His stories and his suggestions will help librarians and library boards do the right thing."

—**Rick Ashton**, former City Librarian, Denver Public Library, 1985–2006

"At a time when our public libraries and librarians are increasingly under attack from the censors, James LaRue's *On Censorship* is the book we need to read *now* to understand why, what's at stake, and what we can do about it. His depth of experience, wisdom, and Zen-like equanimity make him the ideal guide on this journey to the center of censorship, along the way illuminating the invaluable role of public libraries in our communities and our fragile democracy."

—**Claudia Johnson**, author of *Stifled Laughter: One Woman's Story About Fighting Censorship*

Praise for *On Censorship*

"Jamie LaRue's writing on book banning and censorship is a clean, sharp compass needle pointing to the truth. Fifteen years ago, LaRue's blog posts about challenges to *Uncle Bobby's Wedding* helped me understand the complex skeins of what challenges are, while laying out a comprehensive response. Now, in *On Censorship*, he takes on every aspect of censorship and shares useful tips on the best ways to cope with demands for it. *On Censorship* is a much-needed guide for authors, librarians, teachers, and for everyone who reads books in this turbulent century."

—**Sarah Brannen**,
author of *Uncle Bobby's Wedding*

"It is a privilege to have watched Jamie LaRue courageously defend the basic tenets of intellectual freedom over the course of his career, and this book deftly details both philosophy and policy. He provides examples of practicing these values as librarians defend rising challenges to deprive our freedom to read. *On Censorship* is a tribute to the quiet courage of librarians and the essential role of the library in the public square. Jamie is a heroic leader in defending and supporting librarians and libraries everywhere."

—**Pam Sandlian Smith**,
Information Entrepreneur

"*On Censorship* relates a masterful story that illuminates a bold and vivid tapestry of hypocrisy and greed, which drives today's cancel culture. James LaRue poignantly recounts his own efforts to counter hundreds of challenges and inspires other fearless librarians to take courageous actions to elevate public engagement, thought and exploration over censorship, fear, and ignorance."

—**Nancy Kranich**, past President, American Library Association, and Teaching Professor, Rutgers University School of Communication and Information, Department of Library and Information Science

On Censorship

*A Public Librarian
Examines Cancel Culture in the US*

James LaRue

Fulcrum Publishing
Wheat Ridge, Colorado

Library of Congress Cataloging-in-Publication Data

Names: LaRue, James, 1954- author.
Title: On censorship : a public librarian examines cancel culture in the US
 / James LaRue.
Description: Wheat Ridge, Colorado : Fulcrum Publishing, [2023] | Series:
 Speaker's corner books
Identifiers: LCCN 2023011514 (print) | LCCN 2023011515 (ebook) | ISBN
 9781682753477 (paperback) | ISBN 9781682754580 (ebook)
Subjects: LCSH: Libraries--Censorship--United States. | Censorship--United
 States. | Intellectual freedom--United States. | Cancel culture--United
 States. | BISAC: POLITICAL SCIENCE / Censorship | LITERARY
CRITICISM /
 Books & Reading | LCGFT: Essays.
Classification: LCC Z711.4 .L37 2023 (print) | LCC Z711.4 (ebook) | DDC
 025.2/13--dc23/eng/20230518
LC record available at https://lccn.loc.gov/2023011514
LC ebook record available at https://lccn.loc.gov/2023011515

Cover design by Kateri Kramer

Unless otherwise noted, all websites cited were current as of
the initial edition of this book.

Printed in the United States
0 9 8 7 6 5 4 3 2 1

Fulcrum Publishing
3970 Youngfield Street
Wheat Ridge, Colorado 80033
(800) 992-2908 • (303) 277-1623
www.fulcrumbooks.com

*To Maddy and Max, for their curiosity,
kindness, and humor.*

To Sharon, for her counsel and companionship.

*To my fellow librarians and citizen trustees, whose
courage and service we so desperately require.*

*To readers everywhere, whose freedom to read is
enshrined in the First Amendment,
if they can keep it.*

On Censorship

I.
The Role of the Library

My Censored Life

I wish I didn't have so much experience with censorship issues. On the one hand, it's been a handy skill set throughout my library career. On the other, developing that skill meant hanging out with some very angry people.

From 1990 to 2014, I served as director of the Douglas County (Colorado) Public Library District. During that time I personally responded to about 250 challenges. By "challenges" I mean public attempts to remove or restrict access to various library resources. By "responding" I mean reviewing the entire resource, consulting library policies (adopted by the citizen Board of Trustees), deciding about the disposition of the challenged item or resource, and communicating that to the complainant. This response is called a Request for Reconsideration process, and it usually ends with an optional appeal to the board.

Mostly, the targets of challenges were books. But I also fielded attempts to remove or restrict access to magazines, movies, music, programs, displays, artwork, and digital databases—virtually anything a library provides. The good news: my library district checked out more than eight million items in 2014 alone, and had more than four million visits to our buildings and website. So "challenges" represented only a tiny fraction of public use—which is still true today. The not-so-good news: those challenges often came from extremely vocal and influential people in the community. At the beginning, the complaints originated almost exclusively from the political and religious right. Over time, I saw challenges from parents across the political and religious spectrum, for reasons I'll get to later in this book (see "Why People Challenge Library Resources").

From 2016 to 2018, I worked for the American Library Association (ALA) as the executive director of the ALA's Office for Intellectual Freedom (OIF), which was founded in 1964. Many countries have library associations; however, ALA is the only one to have a dedicated office for resisting censorship. During my tenure at ALA, our office tracked and responded to around a challenge a day. In my almost three years there, this meant exposure to almost nine hundred attempts to block access to information. I also wrote OIF's Field Report summary for all publicly reported challenges the following year. This national dataset differed from my Douglas County experience in several ways, unearthing a more generic panic over national demographic and cultural shifts.

In 2022, I took another public library director position, this time on Colorado's Western Slope, which serves six rural communities. In my first eight months, I faced five challenges. Three of them reflected the huge shift in public challenges that the OIF has highlighted since 2020. Rather than being individual complaints, these were coordinated campaigns—often with an overtly partisan, Republican bias—likely designed to rouse the conservative base in time for the 2022 midterm elections.

All told, throughout my career as a defender of free speech and public access to knowledge in all its varied forms, I have dealt with more than a thousand attempts by the public to censor the library. It has always been interesting. It hasn't always been fun.

Why People Challenge Library Resources

Every time I see the barrage of news photos or video clips of human faces distorted by anger, disgust, or outrage (imagine a sputtering Alex Jones in full rant), I think, "This is not an attractive look." Why, then, do some people take it upon themselves to seek to silence others, dismantle longstanding public institutions, and make threats of personal and political violence?

One of them is the self-centered perspective: the idea that one's own perspective is more important, more correct, than anyone else's. I understand.

Why I Hate Brussels Sprouts

Brussels sprouts offend me.

When I was a child, my swing-shift boiler operator dad often cooked dinner. My mother, a nurse, usually worked the midnight shift at a Veteran's Hospital. When dad cooked, we five kids got a slab of grilled rare steak, a glob of potato, and a vegetable (usually from a can). To my father, a child reared in the Depression, this is what prosperity looked like.

One night my dad served us brussels sprouts. They smelled bad, like old cabbage. The taste was disgusting. I bit into one and spat it out.

My dad's rule was that you couldn't leave the table till you cleaned your plate. I slid one brussels sprout under the table. (We once had a dog named Spunky; it may have been brussels sprouts that killed him.) I tried to disguise these evil little cabbage boils under potato skins. But over time, they got cold. I had to stay till I chewed and swallowed them all.

I hate brussels sprouts. The memory fills the back of my throat with bile, makes my eyes water. I am filled with resentment and anger.

One day, while walking through the frozen aisle at the grocery store, I saw a bunch of packages with clear labeling: brussels sprouts.

I went up to the store manager, whom I knew. "Brussels sprouts offend me!" I told him. "Don't I deserve the right to come into a store and not see a product that offends me?"

He thought about it.

Then he said, "Nobody comes to the grocery store because it *doesn't have* what they *don't want.*" He paused. "Some people like brussels sprouts."

It's the same with a library. There are many other choices for my time and attention. I could work to eliminate the mere presentation of obviously offensive, morally repugnant vegetables—I mean books. But some people want them, and I am not actually charged with telling everybody else what they're not supposed to like.

When brussels sprouts kill you (R.I.P. Spunky), I'll be back with some hard evidence. I may push for legislation.

Mostly, though, I think what you don't care for, you can avoid.

Life Transitions
A second reason people seek to censor concerns the shaky moments of parenthood.

Philosophies of child-rearing shift over time. According to the generational analysis of Strauss and Howe (see *Generations*), Baby Boomers were indulged in childhood, Gen-Xers were almost abandoned ("latch-key children"), Millennials were closely supervised, and Gen-Zs were almost smothered—a cycle of loosening then tightening protectiveness. Since the mid-1990s to the present, the cycle has been tightening fast: a shift from "helicopter" to "Velcro" parents.

Having kids rewires the adult brain. We remember things long forgotten, wisps of childhood cluelessness and magical thinking we group under the concept of innocence. We put our adult bodies and sensibilities between our child and the wide world, a task made more urgent by sensational news stories of abductions and abuse.

Daddy's Roommate and Woods without Wolves

That struggle—to ensure an imagined innocence, and to fend off the darker or more complicated sides of adult life as long as possible—tends to sharpen at two distinct periods in the child's life. The first is the transition from toddlerhood to childhood—ages four to six. In most American families, that's the end of the bubble of parental control. Now comes exposure to play dates and daycare and preschool.

Many challenges to public libraries focus on picture books that deal with topics uncomfortable to some parents. In Douglas County, *Daddy's Roommate* (about a man who leaves his wife and child to live with another man), made one patron so upset that they tore up the pages of the book into thirds and threw it on the library floor. But as I explained in a newspaper column I wrote at the time, we had bought the book because a local patron, whose husband had left her for another man, was trying to find a way to talk about this with her young son. We bought the book at her request to help her.

Mary Jo Godwin, former editor of the late *Wilson Library Bulletin,* once wrote: "A truly great library has something in it to offend everyone." But libraries don't buy books *in order* to offend. We buy them to support our community. It surprises some people that not everyone wants the same thing.

As I also explained in my newspaper column, books sparking such destructive attempts to silence a voice are probably needed, and perhaps urgently so. So I announced that following this vandalism, we would buy six *more* copies of *Daddy's Roommate*, which did seem to stop further physical attacks against the book.

But even more frequently challenged were . . . fairy tales.

I once experienced two challenges to *Little Red Riding Hood* on the same day. In one version the Woodman shows up just in time to save Little Red. Then he slices open the wolf, and Granny emerges, whole. In the final scene Granny and the Woodman were having a glass of wine. The complaint: Granny is a drunk; the library was promoting senior alcoholism. My response to the patron was that if I had just been sliced out of a wolf, I'd want a drink, too. Granny had had a day.

In the second version, Little Red, too, was eaten by the wolf. In the final scene, she is floating in the belly of the wolf, suffused with a golden glow. At the door is the shadow of the Woodman. The complaint: "I didn't read this to my daughter because it might have scared her."

In the original fairy tale, of course, neither Granny nor Little Red made it. There was no Woodman. The point of the story was "don't talk to strangers."

At one level, parents get it. They know that it's normal and natural to want to explore the world. And that frisson of fear—the Big Bad Wolf in *Little Red Riding Hood*—is part of the *thrill* of exploration. The woods are lovely, dark, and deep. Parents understand their allure. But the needs of the parent are not the needs of the child. The parent wants woods without wolves. The child needs to know how to deal with wolves.

So some parents react to threatened separation— the child that no longer wants to be carried, or even held too closely—with deep emotion. It's love and loss and grief. Parents want the clock to stop, to rewind. They believe that if they just don't talk about life's complexities, those complexities will never surface.

Uncle Bobby's Wedding

In 2008, I fielded a challenge that came both privately, in the form of a Request for Reconsideration form submitted directly to the library, and publicly, through a much more combative letter to the editor, about the children's picture book *Uncle Bobby's Wedding*, written and illustrated by Sarah S. Brannen. It's an altogether beguiling story about Chloe, a female guinea pig whose favorite uncle, Bobby, is getting married . . . to another male guinea pig. The emotional center of the book didn't really have much to do with gay animals. It focused on Chloe's fear that she would lose her special relationship with a beloved family member. It all ends happily, with Chloe serving as a flower girl in the wedding.

In the Request for Reconsideration, the patron objected that "the book is specifically designed to normalize gay marriage and is targeted toward the two- to seven-year-old age group." Her second concern was that she found it "inappropriate that this type of literature is available to this age group." In my written response, I agreed with her first point. The gay wedding was incidental to the story; it wasn't portrayed as disturbing to anyone. The issue was the relationship between Chloe and her uncle. The book was also, as a juvenile picture book, undeniably written for the preschool to early reader age group. Most juvenile picture books have a colorful illustration on every page, simple language, a relatively straightforward story, and some relatable issue or issues. What defines a children's book is not the content; it's the format.

I disagreed that the book was inappropriate. Even in 2008, gay marriage was legal in many states (although the law remains silent about marriage between guinea pigs of any gender). While she might have found *Uncle Bobby's Wedding* a poor fit for her family, there were other library users who were grateful to find it. The library, paid for by the whole community, also has to serve the whole community.

In her letter to the editor, the patron's tone was more strident. She asked, "Don't I have the right to complain about this book?" She did. The First Amendment doesn't require that you agree with everything you read. As anyone who has been in a book club knows, the most boring meetings are the ones where everyone likes the work. But then she asked, "Don't I have the right not to be offended by things I find in a public library?" And here, as I responded to her in my own letter to the paper, the answer is "No." No such right exists in the Constitution, Amendments to it, or state statute. Indeed, such a right would be unenforceable. In my life I've learned that even the most innocuous things are offensive to some people (see "Why I Hate Brussels Sprouts," earlier). The presumption here is that one person's offense requires someone else to . . . do what, exactly? Say things they don't believe? Shut up? That seems a far more heavy-handed response than simply ignoring what doesn't interest you in the first place, or writing your own book from another perspective.

Douglas County was the first library to receive a challenge to Brannen's book, but I was pretty sure there would be others. So I wrote a blog post about it, withholding the name of the patron, but including my full written response to the challenge.[1] To my surprise, the blog post received many comments. At this writing, there are over 450. The comments fell into several categories: largely complimentary about my response, harshly critical of any positive portrayals of homosexuality, and general comments about the larger role of the public library.

My favorite response from a reader was "We can't childproof the world. We have to worldproof the child."

In response to one of the angrier comments, I wrote, "So much of what passes for discourse these days seems to be nothing more than the rhetoric of rage. It comes down to this: attack, before investigation, before simple inquiry, in lieu of simple courtesy. Impute absurd and sinister motives. Demand that the propaganda cease! Unless it's your own propaganda, which is sacrosanct. Claim your rights as a taxpayer to dictate which views may be promulgated—ignoring that you are not the only taxpayer, and that other taxpayers have different views, and often conflicting demands."

I retained the book. *Uncle Bobby's Wedding* went on to become one of the most frequently challenged books in the country.

The Wonder Years

The second transition is from the end of childhood to the beginning of adulthood. Call it ages fourteen to sixteen. Now, causing even more parental anxiety, the "child" is frankly curious about the adult world. In America, with its puritanical obsession with sex, few threats seem more urgent. But that sex-centric fear often masks deeper issues. The most frequent challenge brought against Toni Morrison's *Beloved* is "graphic sexual content." Like most censorship attempts, this profoundly diminishes the real themes of the book. *Beloved* isn't about gratuitous sex, or prurient frolicking. It's about the very real horrors of slavery, socially sanctioned rape, and systemic dehumanization based on race. The attempt of parents to prevent the teaching of such topics to "children" in their last year of high school—a year before they can serve in the military, marry, or vote—is also a diminishment, an attempt to re-infantilize the young adult. Withholding or canceling these books won't resolve the legacy of slavery, or any of the other issues discussed in Advanced Placement English classes. But it might well dump minors at the door of adulthood less well-equipped to make sense of the world around them.

Another recurrent theme of challenges to young adult materials is language. Parents who have sworn like sailors for decades suddenly object to seeing that cursing in print, even when those words are definitely used by actual young adults.

Many censors of young adult materials fail to take into account two things worth mentioning: not all minors are six years old, and all minors have minds, often quite good ones. Some of the most insightful and probing comments I've ever heard, about many complex topics, have come from minors, including my own children. Age does not reliably confer either maturity or intelligence. Many kids are way smarter than adults think they are, and sometimes more level-headed than the adults around them. They can handle reading a book. (See "Seven Things You Can Do," point #3—"Read More Books and Talk about Them.")

In my view, good parents inoculate their children against physical diseases. In much the same way, books allow children to develop imaginative antibodies. Which is safer: to encounter drugs, sexual pressure, or antisocial behavior in a book, or on the street?

When I was director of the Douglas County Libraries, a woman requested that we buy a book about the Armenian Holocaust (*Forgotten Fire*, by Adam Bagdasarian). We did, and cataloged it as a young adult novel, as the main protagonist was at the transition of childhood to adulthood. After the woman read *Forgotten Fire*, she then requested that we remove it, or at least put it in the adult collection. The story truly was appalling: children watched their parents and siblings get marched out of the house and shot in their front yard; some children were raped. But removing a book about crimes committed against children doesn't stop them from happening. My then fourteen-year-old daughter and I read and talked about it together, and I found myself thinking that it just might have prepared her better to survive—unless we can assure children that such things will never happen again. And we can't.

Mostly, reading is *not* the practice of poring over hard, "sensitive," "problematic," or "inappropriate" topics. But sometimes it is, and that just might be what a child most needs to know. Incidentally, in my experience those words in scare quotes are often semantically null. They seem to be used to indicate "bad" without having to take the trouble to explain *why* they're bad. Objections are often both very emotional and largely unexamined. The vagueness sometimes makes it hard to respond to a challenge. The challenge is in the subtext.

Demographic and Cultural Change

A third source of censorship became plain to me when I worked at ALA's Office for Intellectual Freedom. One of the ALA's most media savvy campaigns is Banned Books Week (BBW), held annually, usually in the last week of September. Created in 1982, BBW was a combined effort of the ALA and various booksellers. It highlighted the surprising fact that some of America's bestselling titles were also among those most frequently challenged in America's libraries.

The first display, at a book exposition in California, set the standard: a bunch of attractive books were cordoned off and surrounded by yellow tape. It was a crime scene. Step under the tape and you could read why the book was challenged.

The enduring appeal of BBW is simple: your favorite book, the one that changed your life, the one that you loved, is sure to be on the list. For many people this is both baffling and astonishing. Why does somebody want to ban *Anne Frank: The Diary of a Young Girl*? Answer: somebody thought the book was "kind of a downer." And what would the result of the banning be? Do we forget Anne Frank?

To this day, the annual list of the Top Ten Most Challenged Items remains the most visited part of the ALA website. The media is fascinated by it, as we always are by forbidden fruit. ("Ooh, what don't they want me to know about?")

One of the responsibilities of the OIF is to track reported challenges from around the country, fielding those reports from school, public, and academic libraries. On the one hand, once again the number of challenges is a minuscule percentage of the materials checked out by library users. On the other hand, various research projects in Missouri, Oregon, and Texas proved that the OIF simply doesn't hear about most challenges, particularly in areas where the items are successfully banned. (The range was from 3 percent reported challenges in Texas, to 18 percent in Oregon.) **Censorship is most effective when nobody talks about it.** So the Top Ten Most Challenged Items list, and the number of challenges generally, isn't a comprehensive public research database. I think library challenge reports are more like smoke in the forest. OIF is a fire spotter, watching the trends, the visible signs of censorship that may augur future conflagration. (In 1934, Sigmund Freud, a Jew, responded to the book burning by Nazis with this statement: "What progress we are making. In the Middle Ages they would have burnt me. Now they are content with burning my books." But they weren't. They never are.)

By the time I joined the OIF (in January 2016), a pattern of challenges had become luminously clear. The challenges across America were overwhelmingly to books by or about LGBTQ+ people, or people of color.

That raises an uncomfortable insight. I would say that the primary clientele of America's public libraries is white straight women between the ages of thirty-five and fifty, and almost half of our business is the book they choose for their children. While on occasion we would hear about a Black mom challenging *Huckleberry Finn* because of its use of the N-word, or *To Kill a Mockingbird* because of its propagation of the White Savior trope, challenges by minorities were rare. That may change. For now, however, America's censorship attempts mostly come from current demographic majorities seeking to suppress writings based on the experiences of current demographic minorities. I'll explore this idea later in the book (see "A Theory of Librarianship").

I learned about three other important aspects of censorship while at ALA.

First, there was a rising trend of individuals, frustrated by the resistance to censorship by their local schools (those fortunate enough to have Request for Reconsideration policies in place), who sought to accomplish through laws what they could not accomplish through local activism. Examples include the "Beloved" bill in Virginia, the "Don't Say Gay" bill in Florida, and the anti-Critical Race Theory Bill in Texas. Often the bills or their authors cite "parental rights" as their guiding principle—but these are parents seeking to impose their views on other people's children.

The second thing I learned is that it's not just librarians fighting against censorship. We have partners. Among them are the American Civil Liberties Union, the Comic Book Legal Defense Fund, the Foundation for Individual Rights and Expression, the Freedom to Read Foundation, the Media Coalition, the National Coalition Against Censorship, and PEN America. Each of these nonprofits addresses the attempts to limit access to ideas or their expression. All of them are worthy of support.

Such groups are essential. In 2022, two books—*Gender Queer* and *A Court of Mist and Fury*—were challenged as obscene under an old Virginia law, the first obscenity prosecution case I'm aware of in more than fifty years that might have affected library practices. This attempt by a Republican state delegate on behalf of another Republican former delegate to declare two bestselling books obscene and unlawful to sell to minors was intended to set a new legal strategy. It failed when the judge found the old law in violation of the First Amendment. Bringing that case to court, and winning it, required a strong coalition of many players.

A third thing I witnessed at the OIF was the rise of a new value in American society: social justice.

In 1985, the Cooperative Children's Book Center (CCBC), School of Education, at the University of Wisconsin–Madison, set out to analyze the number of children's books published in a year, versus the number written by Black authors and illustrators. That year, roughly twenty-five hundred books were published (by mainstream houses), of which eighteen were by Black creators. That's 0.72 percent. By contrast, approximately 11.7 percent of Americans were Black in that year. By 2017, the CCBC estimated about thirty-seven hundred children's books, with 32 books by (.86 percent), and 355 (9.59 percent) about Black people. At that time, Blacks were around 18 percent of the population.

So it looked like progress, when, in 2016, Scholastic published *A Birthday Cake for George Washington*, written by Ramin Ganeshram and illustrated by Vanessa Brantley-Newton, both Black creators. Ganeshram is Trinidadian-Iranian and Brantley-Newton is African American. The book was about Hercules, "America's first celebrity chef."

Hercules was an enslaved member of George Washington's household. During an embargo of sugar by the British, Hercules was tasked with making a birthday cake for the man who would become our first president. Hercules, shown in the kitchen with his daughter, where they exchanged many loving glances, succeeds by substituting honey. In the afterword, the author explains that although Washington intended to free his slaves upon his death, Martha did not. He "belonged" to Martha. So Hercules escaped. In subsequent coverage, it was revealed that Hercules's daughter was once asked how she felt about her father abandoning her. "At least he's free," she said.

I would submit that this is a nuanced story, revealing a slice of American history not known to many. It was a book about an African American, written, illustrated, and even edited by Black women. That expands our understanding of the human story.

At first, the reviews were positive. But soon, a social media campaign (#smilingslaves), mostly spearheaded by African Americans, portrayed the book as trying to show that slavery wasn't all that bad. I would have said, rather, that the book showcased the resilience of enslaved people. It was a story centered in lived Black life, not just of oppression but of family. But both author and illustrator were attacked on social media repeatedly and often viciously. Ganeshram was told she wasn't really Black, so had no business writing about Black experience. Brantley-Newton was told that her warm, tender illustrations were "offensive." In the controversy, Scholastic pulled the book from the market. On the day that was announced I ran over to a local bookstore to see if I could nab a copy. They were all gone. Because of a 1979 decision preventing companies from writing off unsold inventory on their taxes (*Thor Power Tool Co. v. Commissioner*), I suspect the books were destroyed.

I wondered at the time how willing Scholastic would be to offer another book to that team, or tackle other works by or about people of color.

When I talk about this to public audiences, I ask, "Is this censorship?" Most people say it is. They get thoughtful when I ask if they would have the right to pull their own book if the criticism proved damaging to their business. Who owned *A Birthday Cake for George Washington*? Scholastic. Did anyone attempt to prevent the publication of the book, or sue the publisher for running afoul of the law, or require the publisher to pull it? No. So was the withdrawal of the book from the market an act of censorship?

I don't think so. Does the social atmosphere of our time incline toward the willful suppression of books perceived as either insufficiently or *too* woke? I think it does. Might that *lead* to censorship? Absolutely. (For more about who does the censoring, see "On the Media").

I have had many conversations with ALA colleagues about the tension between the more established value of intellectual freedom (see "Library Bill of Rights") and the rising value of social justice. Is there room in

librarianship, or in American society, for both values?
Of course there is.

What Do Libraries Buy and Why?

Library collections have three sources: what's available (i.e., what gets published, mostly by the "Big Five"
publishing houses that dominate the American book
market: Penguin Random House, Hachette, Harper-
Collins, Macmillan, and Simon & Schuster), what gets
well-reviewed (usually by other librarians who recommend a book for a certain kind of library or audience),
and what our patrons ask for.

And what do our patrons ask for?

One thing they want is to see their own lives
and perspectives represented. If LGBTQ+ folks or
people of color come into the library and find nothing or almost nothing about their own stories, they
conclude, "This institution is not for me." Given the
predictions for ongoing demographic shifts, that
could easily turn into an existential institutional cri-
sis. As previously noted, many public institutions are

already under attack. Censorship is one strategy to make libraries irrelevant to tomorrow's America.

The second kind of resource library patrons are looking for concerns things that are *not* about them. My friend Heather was raised by a nationally known storyteller. Her mom, of Scottish descent, regularly brought Heather to the library and checked out all kinds of books. But the first significant book that caught Heather's eye was a collection of African folktales. She loved it passionately, and it sparked a lifelong interest. Eventually she actually went to Africa, collecting more stories. Heather returned to become an acclaimed storyteller herself.

Sometimes the lessons in our lives don't come from our own culture or time. They come from somewhere else, and they can open up new life possibilities. Shutting down either of these directions of exploration shuts down human potential.

Library patrons are looking for more than two things, naturally. They also look for things to educate, entertain, inspire, and distract them. But in the end, the quest is still about identity—who are we in the world, and what should we be doing?

Does Anything Go?
The "Harmful to Minors" Argument

The older I get, the more difficult I find it to hold absolute views about anything, including free speech. Online threats, public health misinformation, and both personal and institutional harassment seem to me reasonable objects of regulation.

Again, much of the public debate around censorship cloaks itself in the language of resources that are "harmful to minors." Adults do have the responsibility to oversee the safety of their children. But let's be clear about the threats.

At this writing, the leading cause of childhood death is firearms. Reading doesn't kill anybody. On the contrary, I would argue that it increases the likelihood of human survival.

Another threat—sexual abuse—is also real. The greatest cause of it, however, is not the library. Most sexual abuse comes from family members. It has also come, as is well documented, from faith communities, as I will address in more detail later. The attempt to shift responsibility from family and church to public institutions is rank hypocrisy. Moreover, the best protection against attempts to sexually exploit children is not ignorance. It is knowledge, often provided by the schools and libraries now under attack.

Yet there are many kinds of injury. Challenges to our deepest beliefs can be shocking and painful. Insults hurt.

The great value of literacy is examination of the world from a distance. Reading gives us the space to process, to consider and test, to assess personal and societal consequences, to formulate a response to ideas and actions.

Earlier I said that the attempt to keep books away from children not only disregards the intelligence of the child; it overlooks the fact that most children aren't interested in adult content—until they are. And when they are, they're ready, to the limit of their understanding. And what goes over their heads doesn't hurt them. To the parents who want us not to buy books about non-straight children, I wonder what they think such children should do. Are *they* not harmed by calumny and neglect? Bigotry and ignorance serve predators, not their prey.

There are many problems in America. Here's something that is *not* a problem: children reading too much.

Libraries, bookstores, and most entertainment media organize their offerings by audience. We don't have to protect children from stories with LGBTQ+ characters. The books won't make them gay, any more than reading mysteries will make them murderers. We read for information and entertainment, and the process of personal change takes longer than reading a single book.

We protect our young by taking action on real, not manufactured threats. We protect children by informing them, by honoring the dignity of their curiosity not with deception but with evidence.

The Surge: 2021–2022

While my own experience both in Douglas County and at the OIF revealed that, on occasion, there were some centrally organized censorship campaigns, usually launched by conservative Christian groups (See "On Religion"), most of the challenges were one-offs, individuals upset to find something in a public place that they personally disapproved of. But in 2021, there was a distinct surge of a different kind of censorship attempt. As referenced by MSN.com, "There were nearly as many 'challenges' between September 1 and December 1, 2021, as ALA normally tracks in an entire year."[2] One of the precipitating events was the action of then Texas Republican state representative Matt Krause. On October 25, 2021, he wrote a letter to the Texas Education Agency in which he asked the agency to report, about every school district in the state,

- How many copies of each book (out of a list of 850 titles) each state district possessed and at what campus locations, including school library and classroom collections, could be found.
- The amount of funds spent by each district to acquire the books.
- Any other books or content, specifying the campus location and funds spent on acquisition, "that address or contain the following topics: human sexuality, sexually transmitted diseases, or human immunodeficiency virus (HIV) or

acquired immune deficiency syndrome (AIDS), sexually explicit images, graphic presentations of sexual behavior that is in violation of the law, or contain material that might make students feel discomfort, guilt, anguish, or any other form of psychological distress because of their race or sex or convey that a student, by virtue of their race or sex, is inherently racist, sexist, or oppressive, whether consciously or unconsciously."[3]

The list, of uncertain provenance, mostly focused on the usual suspects: books by or about LGBTQ+ issues, or people of color. But the list also included books about the Universal Declaration of Human Rights, teen rights, sexual abstinence, Navy Seals, and a grab bag of other topics.

Newspapers and many commentators pointed out that directing school employees to gather this data at the expense of taxpayers is hardly the work of a fiscal conservative. Moreover, the list itself was ideologically incoherent, although it may have been designed more to give visibility to Krause, who was angling for a district attorney job at the time. Whatever the motivation, by

December of the same year a San Antonio school district announced that it had removed four hundred books from its library shelves. The censorship then moved to Texas public libraries, when Llano County libraries shut down for three days so librarians could conduct a "thorough review" of all children's books. They also turned off the service that provided access to ebooks. Soon, other Texas communities followed, especially after Governor Greg Abbott wrote the Texas Education Agency to investigate the availability of "pornographic books" in schools. This direct political pressure not only winds up in the actual removal of books from the school (yes, books are banned); it also establishes a "chilling atmosphere"—a climate of caution, rather than a culture of learning. Seeing which way the wind is blowing, few teachers or librarians will risk buying books that will get them in trouble. And so the censors succeed.

Even more aggressive was Oklahoma Republican state senator Rob Standridge's proposed legislation on December 16, 2021, which would "allow a parent to compel book removals in schools. If the book is not gone within 30 days, the complaining parent could collect at least $10,000 in court, and the librarian could be fired."[4] The Oklahoma bill did not pass. The fact that it was even proposed, however, shows a big shift in the censorship landscape. This was not just parents complaining about books they weren't ready for their kids to read. This was the weaponization of state government to actively purge public institutions of forbidden topics and views. It also focused on punishing those who facilitated access to those views.

Surge Tactics

In 2021 and 2022 many schools and libraries experienced a new round of challenges. In general, the process looked like this:

- The first time that a library staff or board hears about a challenge is at a public meeting.
- Not just one person shows up; it's usually three to five, maybe more.
- Typically it isn't just one book that is challenged; it can be 10 or 20 or 850. It's worth noting that sometimes people have demanded removal of specific books the institution doesn't even own (a children's biography on Michelle Obama), and

requiring the immediate replacement of the title with something that doesn't yet exist (a biography of Melania Trump).

- During public comment sessions, they read aloud the naughtiest passages they can find, focusing (usually) not just on sex, but on gay sex, or sex involving people of color. Often these out-of-context snippets are the only part of the book the speakers have read, and usually have been provided to them by conservative blogs and emails.

- They express anger and shock that such things are available to children in the library.

- They demand immediate action (i.e., the removal of the book or books in question). They threaten political retaliation if the board does not instantly comply. In schools, they threaten to fire the librarian, the teacher, the principal, the superintendent, and to recall the school board. In the case of public libraries, the focus is on firing the librarian, the director, recalling the library board, and defunding the library altogether. That defunding actually happened in Jamestown Township, Michigan, where 56 percent of the voters chose not to renew the property tax that underwrote 80 percent of the library's operations. Why? Those voters strongly protested the presence of LGBTQ+-friendly titles in the library.

Because of a decades-long push to dismantle public institutions of many kinds, it's not surprising that some public administrators shy away from controversy in the first place, or move quickly to make it go away without resolving the underlying issues. Hence, administrators preemptively pull books even before they are challenged.

One example of this was the book *13 Reasons Why* by Jay Asher. Published in 2007, the book was challenged in many school libraries, mainly because of the important and relevant topic of teen suicide. People also objected to teenagers acting like teenagers—the book depicted high school students engaging in sexual behavior and rude language.

Yet it's true, particularly in rural areas, that suicides can be contagious, racing through a high school in just days or weeks. So parents and administrators, from anticipatory fear, tried to pull the book. Librarians largely defended it. The book was well-written, addressed real concerns of young adults, and generated discussion about a current social problem.

In 2017, the Netflix series of the same title came out, and was more disturbingly graphic than the book (whereas in the book the female protagonist kills herself by taking pills, in the TV series she slits her wrists in a bathtub).

Public reaction to the series was mixed. Some people praised its unflinching honesty. Others believed that it failed to provide more positive mental health strategies, focusing too much on the potential causes of suicidal thoughts. In either case, the release of the TV series resulted in renewed challenges to the book. One high school principal in western Colorado simply went into the school library and removed all copies. Local school librarians, however, stood up for the book, pointing out that no challenges had been received, and that policies for review had not been followed. Rather than less information about the topic, they argued, the library should provide *more*. Eventually, the books were returned to the shelf, and the school website added a section for resources to help teens dealing with a host of mental health issues. It was a shining moment for librarianship.

But this would be the exception, not the rule. Many copies of the book simply disappeared in 2017.

In 2018, various #MeToo allegations against the author brought another twist to the story. Now it was librarians who felt compelled to remove the books, just as many staff had quietly pulled Bill Cosby's entirely innocuous children's books after the actor-comedian's conviction of sexual assault. This marked the OIF's first reported challenge of titles not because of content but because of accusations against the author. A more recent example is J. K. Rowling's social media comments about trans women, perceived by some to be insufficiently sensitive to or supportive of LGBTQ+ rights.

On the one hand, it's certainly fair to investigate and consider the prejudices and mindsets of authors. That has long been a legitimate part of literary criticism. On the other, few authors of beloved works are paragons of virtue and inclusiveness. And once again, challenges based on sentiments out of sync with the cultural moment, in fact, diminish the books and the authors. Dr. Seuss's works have been challenged because some alleged his art was derived from illustrations of minstrel shows. Laura Ingalls Wilder's work was accused of anti-Indian bias. Yet Seuss spoke and wrote against racism. Wilder's focus was not on Indian affairs but on self-reliance. Rowling's works mostly center on bravery, family, friendships, and love.

But back to the Surge. The timing and the instigators of the challenges had an overtly political bias. Three groups in particular stirred the pot. The first group was Moms for Liberty, originally formed in Florida at the beginning of 2021 as a conservative group pushing back against school mask mandates during the pandemic, then later going after books. They were known to have strong ties with the Republican Party, both within Florida and beyond. The GOP was the second group, aided and abetted by Fox News and conservative radio. The third group was Catholicvote.org, another conservative group (not directly affiliated with the Catholic Church), which used the language of religious liberty to seek to impose private religious values on public institutions.

At this writing, it's now clear that the Surge isn't over. But to be clear, it was not some grassroots movement of popular consensus. It was more like the Tea Party, a frankly political and nationally coordinated campaign. The purpose of the Surge, based on timing and messages, was to gin up enough fear, anger, and campaign contributions to drive Republicans to the polls in time for the 2022 midterm elections. But there will be other elections.

The Importance of Public Engagement

But there was another shift. Whereas most libraries have dealt with censorship challenges more or less directly—an administrator responding in writing to a complainant—many of these surges were met with genuine grassroots pushback. My current library is an example.

A patron showed up at a board meeting to protest a particular manga series (Japanese anime–style novels). He felt that the series was pornographic, and the books did indeed show drawings of men having sex with each other. There is a style of manga called Yaoi, which is a genre of fictional media featuring homoerotic relationships between male characters. Interestingly, the genre is typically created by women for women.

Originally, our complainant said he didn't believe in banning books. He just wanted us to put the books high enough, "on the top shelf," so a six-year-old child couldn't reach them. (I had told him that six-year-olds really weren't interested in the complex storylines and artwork of adult manga. He didn't believe me, but then, he'd never had any kids.) He also made various misrepresentations about the title: it was "man/boy pedophilia." (No, it wasn't; all the characters in the series were adults.) "It should be cataloged as an adult book." (It always had been.) "There should be a label on the book warning off parents." (A parental advisory label was printed on the cover by the publisher. Our library also stuck a label on it indicating that it was not shelved with young adult manga.) "It had been part of a month-long Pride display." (It may have been, briefly, but if so, it wasn't the staff who put it there.)

He had not at that time filed a formal complaint. But when we failed to withdraw the books or move them to some less accessible location, he started recruiting people to the library board meetings. In the end, he rounded up five or six people, and gathered letters from a couple others, including his priest, all calling for the books to be restricted or removed. The people that came to the meetings followed the national script. They repeated the misrepresentations. They found and relished the reading of the naughty bits of several other books. One person claimed we were violating a state law (about disseminating pornographic material to minors) that turned out to have been found unconstitutional in 1985. Others said I should be fired for my failure "to protect the children." Still others demanded that the library board itself resign. Yet another called for the defunding of the library, just like in Michigan (which he cited). Another referenced other books from ALA's own frequently challenged list that she believed should be banned as well (*Gender Queer* and *This Book Is Gay*). The original complainant hardened his stance: it was no longer enough to put the books on the top shelf. Now, he said out loud that he thought they should be burned. (I should report that some of his previous supporters visibly recoiled.)

Just weeks prior to this incident, a similar scenario had taken place in Wellington, Colorado, in which the lead complainant was the wife of the library board president. She had a list of some fourteen to nineteen titles she wanted removed. Quietly, the library director and others put out a call to the community. When many more people showed up at the board meeting to speak in favor of books about more marginalized populations than showed up to support censorship, the board made a surprising decision: they voted to ban banning. To my knowledge, such a thing hadn't happened before anywhere in America.

One of the speakers in Wellington who protested the attempt to suppress books about gay people asked an intriguing question: "Is this how we want to be known?"

In other words, there was a shift from administrative responses to individual complaints, to a community-wide discussion, playing out in the public library, about community identity. It should be noted too that many of the speakers against censorship were under thirty years old, and often under twenty.

As we are seeing in national politics generally, the rising generations, themselves far more diverse than any of their predecessors, roundly reject homophobia and racism.

At my library, the community also got word about the attempts to censor library materials. They too showed up not only to speak against banning books, but also in favor of the broadest possible exposure to topics of the day. They spoke approvingly of Black History and Pride Month. The most telling comment in response to the "protect the children" argument came from a particularly well-spoken mom. "I am perfectly capable of supervising my own children," she said. The supporters of the library outnumbered the pro-censorship speakers by 2 to 1.

There is evidence that the urge to purge does tend to be a minority opinion. A survey conducted by ALA, published in March of 2022, showed that 71 percent of respondents (voters and parents) oppose efforts to have books removed from their local public libraries, including majorities of Democrats (75 percent), Independents (58 percent), and Republicans (70 percent). Moreover, it found that most

voters and parents were confident that library workers made good decisions about their collections, and
offered books with broad and diverse viewpoints.
Finally, "Voters across the political spectrum have a
sense of the importance of public libraries (95% of
Democrats, 78% of Independents, 87% of Republicans) and school libraries (96% of Democrats, 85%
of independents, 91% of Republicans)."[5]

The survey reminded me that I had done something similar back in the 1990s. A group of parents,
mostly connected to Focus on the Family (an evangelical radio ministry active in Colorado Springs,
Colorado), told me that they were sure most people in the community supported their attempts to
remove books these parents deemed not "family
friendly." So I too took a survey. I stood outside the
library and handed departing patrons a one-question
sheet. "Some people believe that some materials are
inappropriate for public library collections. What
is your view?" My attempt was to be as unbiased as
possible. If someone wrote, "The library should collect everything it can afford—except X-rated films!"
I counted that as "some materials are inappropriate

for library collections." I received almost five hundred responses, and more than 65 percent of my extremely conservative community said, "No censorship!"

Again, the imposition of censorship is the attempt by the minority to suppress information available to the majority. One response to the Surge has been to open up the topic to the community at large.

What happened at my library about the manga complaints? After the midterm elections, only the original complainant returned. But the midterm elections also took place—it may be that some of the organizing fervor had cooled.

A Theory of Librarianship

This experience with our own little surge was eye-opening. During one of his public comment sessions, the initial complainant said, exasperated, "Why do you need to promote books about gay people anyhow? Why can't you offer books on dating someone of the opposite sex, or starting a family, or raising kids with two parents, man and woman?"

It got me thinking. I then went back and dove into our computer catalog, looking for materials by various keywords. What did we actually have under "gay, homosexual, LGBTQ+" and related terms? And what did we have under such terms as "parenting" or "dating"? Here's what I found: approximately 97 percent of our collection reflected more traditional heterosexual-centered viewpoints. We were doing precisely what the challenger said we should do. We just weren't doing it *exclusively*. About 3 percent of books on related topics reflected the perspective of emerging voices. For some people, 100 percent is barely enough.

The more I've considered this, the more I think it highlights a deeper truth—*libraries span time*. At any given moment, the bulk of the collection reflects the ongoing social consensus. After all, we've been buying materials over many years. The collection will favor those publishers and authors that appeal to existing systems of acquisition (both by editors and by librarians), and distribution (mainstream publishers and jobbers). That means, in 2022, that most of our materials reflect a white, cis-gendered perspective.

Libraries hold up a mirror to our culture, and mostly, both mirror and institution look backward, in the same way that our bodies carry the choices of previous years.

But societies change. Change, by definition, doesn't come from the mainstream. It comes from the fringe. Usually slowly, but sometimes with surprising speed, new voices rise up. At present, library collections have begun to build new collections of emerging voices: the voices of people of color, of LGBTQ+ folks, and of people whose internal wiring isn't "neuronormal." Some of these historically marginalized groups have long lived in the shadows of our culture and have been denied access to publishing platforms for a host of historical reasons.

That 3 percent tends to be the focus of challenges. In the US, overwhelmingly, challenges come from the political or religious right. They demand that libraries preserve the 97 percent, a narrative of privilege and power, and that we silence anyone who dares to critique it. Again, Florida's "Don't Say Gay" law and anti-Critical Race Theory legislation are prime examples.

To a much lesser extent, far less than on the right, there are also challenges from the political or secular left. Libraries should embrace and expand the new voices! And while we're about it, let's go back and purge the voices of oppressors and other "problematic" speech. (As mentioned earlier, some liberal voices seek the removal or replacement of works by Dr. Seuss, Laura Ingalls Wilder, Harper Lee, and J. K. Rowling.)

Libraries are places where we track the times, noting the shifting winds of our society. As I have said many times to challengers, we don't write the books on our shelves. We buy them on your behalf. We sample the topics of the day. Why do we buy books about LGBTQ+ issues or race? Because people are talking about them, because the topics are in the news, on TV, and are being played out in our own families over dinner.

Whether the challenges come from the right or the left, however, at either extreme, they agree. They want the library to endorse and promote only their own views. They seek to erode the explicit institutional mission of the library and replace it with something else: the advancement of their own agendas.

The Institutionalization
of Values

From Citizen to Consumer

As measured by Gallup polls, confidence in many US institutions—including churches, media outlets, political institutions (Congress, the Supreme Court, the presidency), universities, banks, and the police—have mostly fallen over the past forty years. I don't think that's an accident. There has been a longstanding effort to discredit public institutions for many years. We have seen in my lifetime a replacement of the idea of "citizenship" with the idea of "consumption."

Years ago, I attended a meeting of the local Rotary club. A Scoutmaster passed around several older Boy Scout manuals. The oldest Handbook—the fifth printing, published in 1948—featured a striking cover of a transparent Indian chief rising from a campfire. I turned to the section on citizenship, and found this:

What Others Have Done for You

Your heritage has not been won in battles alone. The electric light, the telephone, the many advantages you enjoy are possible because of someone's hard work and sacrifice—for you.

The school you attend was built and is maintained so that you may have a better chance. . . .

Libraries, museums, and other institutions are maintained for your benefit. Scouting experiences are available to you because of the unselfish service of many people eager to help boys.

By the 11th edition of the Boy Scout Handbook, published in 1998, the message had changed:

Every time you run across a playground, visit a museum or a zoo, or read a book in a library, you are using community resources. . . . Of course, a library without readers has no purpose. A zoo without visitors won't stay open long. A concert hall lacking an audience is doomed to close. You can help keep community resources full of life by using them.

Between these two passages I see a profound shift in the perceived value of the public sector. In the first, post–World War II version, the idea is that adults care so much about the opportunities afforded their young that they were willing to sacrifice to build important institutions.

By just before the year 2000, the message about the public sector is this: use it or lose it. Who benefits from this shift? People who sell stuff. Who loses? The government.

I detect other differences as well. Earlier versions of the Boy Scout Handbook focus on responsibilities: your obligations as a citizen, an emphasis on honor, a respect for the labor of your elders. Later versions focus instead on your rights and freedoms—or perhaps only your convenience.

After the bombing of Pearl Harbor, FDR spurred the nation to unite and act collectively. After 9/11, George W. Bush encouraged us to keep shopping.

This is not to say that those were the good old days, and these are the bad. The postwar years were also a time of political machines, McCarthyism, and worse. Nor is it my intent to denigrate the private sector. The American standard of living for many is very good indeed—the innovations and productivity of the private sector is one of the reasons.

But I think our society is heading for trouble in the rising sentiment that all public institutions are inherently coercive, dirty, doomed, or irrelevant. Public service, like private industry, depends upon a pool of talent. As I listen to people chatting in restaurants and coffee shops, it's surprising how often I hear people speak ill of the government, even people who work for the government in some fashion.

If we parents consistently send this message to our children, we not only unravel some important elements of community, we also turn away the best and brightest of the next generation from a possible career in the public sector.

If we succeed, I can guarantee that the next folks who pick up the reins of power will not be good scouts.

But public or private, all institutions have deep purposes. How did libraries come to hold theirs?

Values Change Over Time

Professions are predicated on values. In 1892, the American Library Association was guided by this modest motto: "The best books for the most people at the least cost."

In 1938, the director of the Des Moines Public
Library, Forrest Spaulding, noted that, "Today indications in many parts of the world point to growing
intolerance, suppression of free speech and censorship
affecting the rights of minorities and individuals."[6]
Among those indications was the rise of Hitler in
Germany, Mussolini in Italy, and Stalin in the Soviet
Union. Books under attack in Des Moines eventually included *Mein Kampf* (both for being "foreign,"
and for promotion of anti-Semitism) and *Grapes of
Wrath* (for being "communist"). In response, Spaulding pitched a "Library's Bill of Rights" to his board. In
1939, it was revised and adopted by the council of the
ALA as the Library Bill of Rights. Since then, it has
been adopted by many libraries.

The Library Bill of Rights
The American Library Association affirms that all
libraries are forums for information and ideas, and that
the following basic policies should guide their services.

1. Books and other library resources should be
   provided for the interest, information, and enlight-

enment of all people of the community the library serves. Materials should not be excluded because of the origin, background, or views of those contributing to their creation.

2. Libraries should provide materials and information presenting all points of view on current and historical issues. Materials should not be proscribed or removed because of partisan or doctrinal disapproval.

3. Libraries should challenge censorship in the fulfillment of their responsibility to provide information and enlightenment.

4. Libraries should cooperate with all persons and groups concerned with resisting abridgment of free expression and free access to ideas.

5. A person's right to use a library should not be denied or abridged because of origin, age, background, or views.

6. Libraries, which make exhibit spaces and meeting rooms available to the public they serve, should make such facilities available on an equitable basis, regardless of the beliefs or affiliations of individuals or groups requesting their use.

7. All people, regardless of origin, age, background, or views, possess a right to privacy and confidentiality in their library use. Libraries should advocate for, educate about, and protect people's privacy, safeguarding all library use data, including personally identifiable information.

(Adopted June 19, 1939, by the ALA Council; amended October 14, 1944; June 18, 1948; February 2, 1961; June 27, 1967; January 23, 1980; January 29, 2019. Inclusion of "age" reaffirmed January 23, 1996.)

Thus 1938 to 1939 marked the true beginning of intellectual freedom as a core value of librarianship. It also may have reflected a dawning social justice awareness: People had the right, and perhaps the obligation, to investigate what was going on in the world, the better to prevent human oppression and suffering.

Social justice or social responsibility (an outgrowth of the civil rights movement and student activism), also has a long history in librarianship. ALA's Social Responsibility Round Table has addressed issues of racism and justice since the sixties. But the core tenets of social justice as a rising value in society seem to trace their origin to Critical Race Theory (CRT). In the mid-1970s, CRT was proposed by African American legal scholars. They argued that the history of race relations in the US, poisoned by the enslavement of Africans, was so pernicious and systemic that it constituted a special case; First Amendment protections should not apply to racist speech. Eventually, this area of writing and research generated many of the terms we now use to discuss Equity, Diversity, and Inclusion (EDI): white privilege, unconscious bias, microaggressions, and systemic racism in many institutions, pointedly including the law. CRT also included the need to transform society through principled resistance, through calling out racist or bigoted behavior, and through being better allies to marginalized people.

Just as 1938 had Hitler, Mussolini, and Stalin, today we again see the rise of authoritarian regimes and dictators in Putin, Erdogan, Xi, and even Trump. And just as intellectual freedom had the social context of World War II, followed by McCarthyism, followed by student protests against an unpopular war, social justice has a context as well. In the twenty-first century alone it ranged from anti-Milo Yiannopoulos protests at Berkeley to the Black Lives Matter protests following a series of high-profile murders of Black men, women, and teenagers by police.

Social justice, like intellectual freedom, now has official library committees that embrace the cause, boasts many professional speeches and writings, has established its own office (of Diversity, Literacy, and Outreach Services), and shares emerging best practices.

We Can Share Values and Have Different Priorities

Many intellectual freedom aficionados also value social justice. Many avowed social justice advocates are fiercely opposed to censorship. But even when we share those values, we may not prioritize them the same way.

That can be driven by personal experience (being a Black or Queer librarian), by social context (what is happening as one comes of age), or community politics (municipal or county power struggles, or race relations).

Sometimes, there is certainly tension between the two values, but I do not believe that they are really *opposed.*

The purpose of free speech is greater individual and social freedom, the pursuit of truth and knowledge, and something we talk too little about these days: the

Common Good. Before groups can advocate for a more just society, they must have the ability to meet, to speak, and to plumb both past and emerging literature. Indeed, that gathering and speaking is part of the advocacy. Others, of course, will advocate for their views, too.

In 1859, John Stuart Mill described free speech as the "marketplace of ideas." His notion was that ideas competed with other ideas, just as products vie with other products. The goal was truth: those ideas that proved more accurate would surely prevail, just as superior products were presumed to prevail in the world of commerce. In 1919, the "marketplace of ideas" language began to be used by the US Supreme Court.

Of course, the superior product does not always prevail, and how are we to explain the rise in 1938, or in 2022, of anti-Semitism and racism, two ideas that have been utterly discredited at every level? It's hard to square Mill with the rise of QAnon, despite its series of inane and improbable predictions that somehow failed to materialize. Perhaps we need only admit that every market has a certain percentage of junk.

**In Libraries, Intellectual Freedom Serves
Social Justice**

I reject the idea that the First Amendment is a tool
of oppression in libraries. The OIF's annual "most
challenged" list reveals the stark truth: overwhelmingly, challenges against American libraries tend to
concentrate on works by or about traditionally marginalized populations. Yet we provide them.

Libraries that have adopted the Library Bill of
Rights, that have a collection policy and a Request for
Reconsideration process, that reach out for support
from the OIF, that more importantly engage the whole
community in the decision, are better positioned to
resist those challenges. In libraries, our policies and
practices do not use the idea of intellectual freedom
to suppress social justice but rather to defend it. This
has been the case since the OIF's founding.

The Importance of Policies and Institutional Purpose

Of the 250 challenges I dealt with in the Douglas
County Public Library District, only three of them

went all the way to the board. Two of those exceptions were simply because I forgot to attach a copy of our policies. Policies, especially when duly adopted by laypeople, present a powerful case to the public. They say, "We thought about this. We know what we stand for." It also helps when a library director can say, truthfully, "Following our policies is my job."

Libraries have many policies, but the key ones relevant to opposing censorship are probably these, formulated by various ALA committees:

- **The Library Bill of Rights**, cited earlier. As noted, this was the foundational document of intellectual freedom for librarians.
- **Code of Ethics**. Here librarians are called upon not only to "uphold the principles of intellectual freedom and resist all efforts to censor library resources," but also to "distinguish between our personal convictions and professional duties and . . . not allow our personal beliefs to interfere with fair representation of the aims of our institutions or the provision of access to their information resources."

- **Collection Development Policy**. Here libraries outline the scope of their collections, and affirm that they seek the broadest possible representation of intellectual content.

- **Programs**. Library-sponsored programs follow the same general thrust as collections: they strive to be broadly representative and nonpartisan.

- **Meetings**. Libraries don't have to make meeting rooms available to the public. Many of them do, however. The policy tends to focus on the fact that once meeting rooms are made available, they must be made available to all, on the same basis. Too, the library does not endorse the views of the people who meet there.

- **Displays.** Libraries also offer space for the exhibition of various things: art, history, hobbies, news, social issues, and more. Again, displays, whether produced by the library or by the community, are more about highlighting current topics or resources than about endorsing them.

- **Internet Access**. The Children's Internet Protection Act, enacted by Congress in 2000, ties the receipt of federal e-rate money (offsetting various telecommunication costs for some schools and libraries), to the use of software filtering, primarily aimed at suppressing access to sexual imagery by minors. The act, as interpreted by the Supreme Court, requires the library to turn off the filtering at adult request. That principle has yet to be tested in court.

- **Patron Behavior**. The focus here is on the distinction between speech and action. When one patron interferes with the quiet enjoyment of the library of another, this policy spells out some consequences: what specific behaviors are not permitted, and what penalties ensue, including ejection from the building, or the summoning of police.

- **Reconsideration.** This approach, whether applied to books or other library resources, is a protocol to thoughtfully examine the object of the challenge in its entirety, weigh it against policy, and make a recommendation for its continuance or restriction.

More generally, policies codify the purpose and operational infrastructure of public institutions. At ALA, I learned that the presence or absence of a robust policy manual was the greatest single determinant of whether a challenged resource is preserved, or censored.

As mentioned earlier, many of the challenges to libraries are attempts to repurpose them, to replace policies with politics. But there's another lesson to holding to policies, an example provided from one of the hot button censorship issues from about 2017 on: drag queen story times.

Does Appeasement Work?

In the rural Midwest, a local drag queen contacted his library. He had been reading about drag queen story times and wanted to give back to his community. Would the library be interested?

A few youth staff visited with the man and found him personable and enthusiastic. He was a skilled makeup artist. The staff talked it over with library administration, and went to visit a drag queen story time at a nearby university town. Judging by the more than two hundred laughing and mesmerized children there, the program was a great success.

So the local library decided to give it a try. They announced the program through all the usual channels. One of those channels was Facebook. Then, in a matter of days, a group of mothers in the area declared themselves outraged. They made eleven phone calls to the director, who had only been on the job and in the community for a few months. In all the calls, the mothers expressed their strong disapproval of the program, which they viewed as the promotion of sexual deviance, and thus "inappropriate" for preschool and elementary school students.

In one of the calls, the director felt the hairs on the back of her neck rise. One of the mothers mentioned casually that she knew where the director lived. At the moment it was hard to tell if that was small town friendliness or almost-threat.

Uncertain and flustered, the director decided that maybe her town "wasn't ready" yet for a drag queen story time. She called the performer and explained that the program would be canceled.

Then she and I had a chance to talk about it.

First, let me admit that public administration can be a highly stressful and isolated life. The director was smart and sincere. Like most of the librarians I meet, she was deeply committed to doing the right thing. But eleven calls about anything in the public sector can feel like a tidal wave. It's easier to listen to people who are speaking than those who are silent. She didn't want to damage the reputation of the library.

Second, I think what she learned, and what I have seen repeatedly in my career, is that *appeasement doesn't work*.

I asked the director, "Do you feel that you won over the folks who called you? Are they now library supporters?" The answer was no. In fact, they watched the library far more closely. They were now convinced of two things. First, the director could not be trusted. Clearly, she didn't know her job. Second, the good news was that she could be bullied into doing the right thing.

But appeasement affected at least two other constituents. The first attempt by the town's Queer community to connect with the library ended in betrayal. It takes a long time to build trust. It can be destroyed in an instant.

A second casualty was the trust of staff. They had diligently explored the option, and gotten approval to proceed. But at the first sign of controversy, their director abruptly undid their work. That trust, too, is hard to get back.

What should the director have done instead?

- Thank the callers for their concern.
- Refer them to policies adopted by the board guaranteeing a broad offering of programs in response to current events and community interest.
- Remind them that attendance at public library programs is voluntary. The programs were clearly advertised and had, in fact, proved popular elsewhere.
- Invite them to propose their own programs. Say that the library belongs to the whole community, and of course not everyone would find each program of interest. Not every program will be successful. This approach, however, does establish that the institution knows its job and walks the talk. That may not win over the eleven mothers, but it does establish a foundation for respect.

Moreover, it builds trust with the many subcommunities of a town. It also sends a clear and supportive message to staff.

Some of the lessons we learn in our professional career are painful. I'm not the first to make a decision I regret. The best response is to learn from those decisions. The takeaway here: our policies articulate our values. Let's not throw them away just because someone yells at us. Let's live them.

How to Respond to Library Challenges

Here are two stories about how I think censorship attempts *should* be handled in libraries.

Princess Buttercup
Ms. Smith (not her real name) came to one of our libraries, where her biracial daughter picked out a book called *Princess Buttercup*. The princess was a fairy, a diminutive creature with wings. To celebrate

her birthday, she interacted with some of her fellow fairy princesses, then wandered off into the forest. When she got lost, a butterfly flew her back to the party. The end.

But on page 9, Princess Iris was neither enthusiastic, nor inclined to help with the party prep. Instead, she was "lazy." She played basketball, tossing the ball through a spider web net. Princess Iris was the only fairy with brown skin.

Ms. Smith approached one of our staff and said she found that page to be a racist stereotype. She believed that providing that book to the community promulgated hurtful biases, and that it was, in fact, damaging to some children.

The staff person followed our protocol. She apologized for an unpleasant experience with the library. She listened carefully to the concern. She said it back to Ms. Smith to make sure Ms. Smith knew the staff person got it. She offered alternative service. But when the patron didn't want to let the issue go, the staff person offered the Request for Reconsideration. And in that Request, Ms. Smith requested that the item be removed.

As part of my review of the item, I did something I usually didn't do. I called, then wrote the publisher. Who made the decision to make the only lazy fairy Black? The author? The illustrator? Having heard the concern, how would the publisher suggest I talk about the publisher's intent?

The publisher did not respond.

Finally, I wrote Ms. Smith back saying that I agreed with her that both the image and description were racist. Although the library was trying to build a more diverse collection, the industry had a ways to go. That image hadn't been called out in written reviews of the book. But the truth is that there were many depictions of people—in fiction and nonfiction, in adult and children's materials—that reflected the biases of authors, cultures, and times. Even in classic literature—Shakespeare's *The Merchant of Venice*, as an example—there was bigotry. This principle for pulling books had larger implications. I believed that our policies prevented me from removing the title. I pointed out, though, that all books wear out sooner or later, and I doubted that we would replace this one. I informed the patron that the library would be keeping the title in the kid's area. I also told her that she had the right to appeal my decision.

She promptly wrote back saying that she profoundly disagreed with my decision, and did indeed want to appeal it. I put her on the agenda for our next meeting.

At the meeting, our board president (who had once chaired the county's planning commission and was thus no stranger to controversy) greeted her warmly. "Ms. Smith, thank you for coming. We're going to pass our consent agenda, then your issue will be our second order of business." After our consent agenda, he said, "Jamie, please summarize what's happened to date." I did, during which time I said that I thought the issue of racist imagery, particularly in children's books, was an important topic. I said I intended to write about it for my weekly newspaper column. I offered Ms. Smith my column for the following week, to use as she wished. She accepted the offer.

Then our board president asked her to speak. She was focused, specific, and persuasive. "This book is *not The Merchant of Venice*," she said. She expressed her dismay that librarians somehow didn't under-stand the power of early exposure to racism. She repeated that she thought we should not only remove this title, but we should really step up our purchases of more inclusive titles.

The board members, all of whom had read my response, reviewed our policies, and also read the book, then took a roll call vote. All of them agreed that the page was racist and that we should look for more current and inclusive titles. Six of the seven board members, however, felt that our policies con-strained us from censorship, and voted to retain the title. One board member sided with the patron.

Afterward, our president said, "May I ask, Ms. Smith, how you feel you were treated today?" She said, "Well, I don't agree with your decision. But I do understand why you made it."

A month or so later, we had a board vacancy. My board president called me. "Encourage Ms. Smith to apply." I did. Her interview was impressive; she was appointed to the board. Two years later, she went from being our first Black board member, to becom-ing board president.

When she responded to a patron at a board meeting complaining about R-rated videos in the library, she jumped in, "The library is opposed to censorship." She had come to see and embrace the value of intellectual freedom.

About a month after that, she was in a local bookstore when her daughter held up the book. "Look, Mom!" Shaking her head, Ms. Smith picked it up, and glanced at page 9. The story had changed. Now, "Princess Iris made a game for the party."

Here's what I like about the story: at every stage, Ms. Smith was treated with respect. She had a point and was willing to make that point not only to the library board, but to the community (through the newspaper article). She earned a seat at the table, and assumed a leadership role.

In the end, her actions wound up persuading a publisher to replace a racist stereotype with a more positive presentation.

The Muslim Experience

In Darby, Montana, the new library director decided that part of her job was to bring the world to her mostly white, rural, ranching community. Working with the state humanities council, she booked an African American cowboy as the first speaker. He talked about growing up Black in Montana, and what that was like. His experience varied from those of his audience in many respects. But he was a Montanan, and a rancher, too. Nearly twenty-five people showed up, expressing their appreciation.

The second speaker was Chinese American, and he talked about how his ancestors had immigrated to America, helped build the railroad, and then suffered appalling discrimination across the Pacific Northwest. Maybe fifty people showed up for that one.

Then she brought in a professor of Arabic languages who was Muslim. When this was announced, a local veteran who had served in the war in Afghanistan strongly protested. He said he knew that Muslims hated America and wanted to destroy it. Their goal was to proselytize Americans into the faith of Islam. This speaker must not be permitted.

The director invited the veteran to meet with her board. They said they certainly weren't trying to proselytize anyone, but the truth was that most folks didn't know very much about the Muslim faith, although it was in the news. The library was offering an educational program, not a religious or political one.

Unmoved, the protester continued to circulate petitions against the talk.

The director then sought advice from many parties. She talked to the local sheriff, who asked if she wanted an armed guard in attendance at the meeting. The director didn't think that set quite the right tone. She spoke to the fire department, who told her their tiny library could hold no more than about 150 people. She spoke with the local League of Women Voters. She called ALA's OIF.

On the day of the program, the director closed the library at 5:00 p.m. then moved things around to pack in the maximum number of chairs. At 6:30 p.m. she opened the doors to find more than five hundred people waiting to get in—more than 10 percent the population of the county.

She calmly distributed her 150 tickets to the first folks in line. Before the remaining crowd could get restive, her board members came out with plates of fresh cookies and coffee. They made strong eye contact with those who couldn't get into the meeting. "We're so sorry," they said. "Please have a cookie." (Eye contact helps to remind people to behave. That's why Walmart used to have greeters—it reduced theft.)

Once inside, the director distributed five comment cards to all the audience members. If they had questions, they were instructed to write them down and pass them over to the director—a tip from the League of Women Voters about how to keep a question session civil, and not provide an opportunity for someone to give an inflammatory speech in the guise of a question.

Then she welcomed everyone to the library, opening with, "Here in America, land of the free, we're free to believe anything we want. No one can make us believe something we don't. And here in America, home of the brave, we're also not afraid of new ideas. And here in Montana, we believe in something we call Western hospitality. Please join me in welcoming our speaker."

This was a masterful framing of a public conversation, appealing not to either a pro- or anti-Islamic stance but rather to a larger set of shared values.

After the lecture, many people submitted question cards. The director didn't dodge the tough questions and asked them respectfully. At the end of the questions, which ran over the original time period by more than an hour, the director asked for a round of applause for the speaker and got it.

Then the speaker said, "And a round of applause for the librarian who gave us the opportunity to have this conversation." She got a standing ovation.

Later, the local newspaper, which may have anticipated the following day's headline as "Riot Erupts at Community Library," instead ran the headline: "Meaningful Conversation at Local Library." Said one attendee, "It was so refreshing to have a program where we could listen, learn, and engage. We have such a thirst for meaningful conversation."

I believe that most of the people in our communities have the same thirst. Too often in our society people either don't engage at all with gnarly issues or they only talk to people who already agree with them. This problem is particularly severe online, where many of us find ourselves being "in the middle of the road" in territory that is ever more extreme.

The only way out of this contentious trap is to do just what the library did—find knowledgeable and reputable sources of information. Serve as a model in setting some ground rules to allow for true intellectual exploration. Connect people and ideas. Have a meaningful conversation.

II.
Cancel Culture

The True Believer—Everything Returns

As previously noted, there are many causes for censorship (personal preference, parental panic, demographic shifts, and disapproval of the author) in our society. As one pointed example, the attack on the US Capitol on January 6, 2021, felt and was different, as have been the subsequent laws seeking to suppress certain viewpoints from the public square. While I've seen other political and social conflicts in my life, the insurrection fell far outside the pattern of late twentieth century American politics.

The mission to silence the "opposition," to view every argument as an existential conflict between "right" and "wrong" neatly reinforces the thesis of Eric Hoffer's *The True Believer: Thoughts on the Nature of Mass Movement*. Those at the outer edges of a continuum (far political left, far political right) have more in common with each other than they do with the many people in the middle. Published in 1951, *The True Believer* grappled with the question that haunted many World War II survivors: How did it happen that the world's geopolitical landscape could lapse so abruptly first into dogmatism and absolutism and then, inevitably and perhaps cyclically, into genocide and destruction?

Does the rapid growth of censorship in our nation, the surge of unhinged social media, the eruptions of real and threatened violence, mark the beginning of a dark mass movement?

In general, Hoffer concluded that times of sudden and alarming shifts in global politics depended on a host of dysfunctions. Societies lose the confidence that comes from a unifying narrative, of underlying consensus and direction. Prior to World War II the belief in free market capitalism was shaken by the Depression in the US, and by crippling war reparations for post–World War I Germany. There began to be what Hoffer calls "the 'new poor,' who throb with the ferment of frustration."[7] These many frustrated minds, in his view, are the seeds of mass movements.

In our own time, the top 1 to 5 percent in America is doing quite well. Everyone else's wages have stagnated for decades. *Hillbilly Elegy* by J. D. Vance is one example of the belief that today's America is dystopian, rigged against the "little guy," who is trapped in Big Pharma–sponsored addiction and governmental dependency.

In recent years, the mortality rate for white men has fallen, reversing long trends. This has nothing to do with immigration, LGBTQ+ rights, or affirmative action, though many think it does.

At the core of today's angry conservatives is aggrievement, anger at the sheer unfairness of their loss of privilege, as if privilege is a zero-sum game. For many angry progressives, the anger is at a long-denied equality, at the fresh memory of oppression.

Another tell in the making of a True Believer is "nationalist fervor," which Hoffer believes is essential to nurture and consummate "revolutionary enthusiasm."

Deutschland Über Alles and America First mean the same thing. Hoffer believes that when people feel aggrieved and dissatisfied in their own lives, they turn to ideals of something bigger than themselves. It often begins as an inchoate hatred of some scapegoat, usually a real or fanciful "foreigner": Jews, immigrants, communists. He notes it is much easier to unite people against the foreign devil than to actually live the precepts of local angels. But with another ingredient—the beginnings of political power—that unifying hatred takes on an evangelical inevitability. A lone gunman showing up at a pizza parlor is a rube. Hundreds of militia members, sporting their rifles and surrounding Michigan legislators from the balcony, is an intoxicating fraternity. It feels like destiny. When the First Amendment meets the Second, it takes a special courage to speak up.

One of our time's contradictions, as articulated in Thomas Frank's *What's the Matter with Kansas? How Conservatives Won the Heart of America*, is the support of mid- to low-income conservatives for policies that not only don't benefit them but instead benefit the elites they claim to despise. Why? Because some people identify with an ethos they imagine allowed the rich and powerful to become so. In the US, having money is self-evident proof both of morality and intelligence. If we only pick out those characteristics we share—we are white, we believe in hard work—then our success is just around the corner. Then we too are powerful, despite our struggles to meet a medical bill or stretch a paycheck.

It may also be that before we can proceed with arrogant confidence to silence others, we must have an extravagant hope in the future. It doesn't have to be true or even reasonable. Many QAnon followers believed that even the dead (e.g., John F. Kennedy, Jr.) would rise to join with Trump in an unbeatable mixture of braggadocio and mythology. Hoffer wrote, "All active mass movements strive . . . to interpose a fact-proof screen between the faithful and the realities of the world."[8] Let's not say "lie." They're "alternative facts."

Earlier, I mentioned the longstanding dismantling of public institutions. Hoffer wrote, "Mass movements do not usually rise until the prevailing order has been discredited. . . . discrediting is not an automatic result of the blunders and abuses of those in power, but the deliberate work of men of words with a grievance."[9]

Today, the role of "militant men of words" is filled by conservative radio and television celebrities. They're looking for traction—and they're getting it. When America faced a literal insurrection—the attempt to prevent the peaceful transfer of power by political violence, predicated on the "Big Lie" of election fraud, it was a handful of ethical people in key public institutions that stymied its success. Institutions are not perfect, but they do tend to perpetuate order and stability. Mass movements don't want stability; after all, people think the system is rigged against them. Followers of such mass movements, or joiners, want the purging release of destruction from which a new order will emerge, spontaneously, with the followers magically elevated to positions of social status and leadership. Hoffer believed that such joiners are frustrated, naturally obedient, and submissive; they are profoundly dissatisfied with the meaninglessness and lack of creativity in their lives. They find purpose and identity through submersion in the movement, a capitulation to the persuasiveness of coercion.

Part of me thinks this kind of analysis comes down to blaming mass movements on psychologically crippled people, manipulated by "men of words," who eventually give way to men of action. (In Soviet Russia, this was the shift from Lenin to Stalin.) There's the potential of another kind of demonization—dismissing anyone *who doesn't agree with you* as damaged mentally or spiritually. But I don't think, in the end, that is Hoffer's point. Rather, the behavior of large groups of people, even if they apparently disagree (e.g., fascists versus communists) start to reveal larger sociological shifts. Hoffer also noted that Hitler found it much easier to recruit people who had already belonged to some grand mass movement (it wasn't hard to turn a communist into a fascist, and vice versa), than people who were more settled and invested in the current order.

My other gleaning from Hoffer is this: destruction is so much easier than creation. He offers some sobering diagnostic principles. When should we worry that we are heading again to world conflict? When collectively people talk about an idealized past and assert that the way to get back to such a place is to burn the current system down without considering what they'll replace it with.

I've never gotten a challenge to *True Believer*. But Hoffer's insights remain as controversial and provocative as they were in 1951.

On Religion

When looked at broadly, censorship overall is made up of four broad dimensions:

1. treason—accusations of disloyalty or treason;
2. obscenity—objections to some sexual descriptions or behavior;
3. blasphemy—contradictions to religious teachings; and
4. bigotry—animus against racial or ethnic groups.

These days, libraries of all types find two topics reliably inflammatory—LGBTQ+ and racial justice. In the first case, the attacks are often based on faith (see "Cherry-Picking the Verses You Like"). Some people are opposed to any expression of human sexuality whether in fiction or sex education curriculum.

They believe their prudery should be public policy. In the second, the rise of anti-Semitism and suspicion of Muslims often hides behind the language of religion, even when it more directly reflects white nationalism. Is religion code for "race?" It can be, or just a cover for other prejudices.

Follow the Money

For a while in the early 1990s, I was receiving close to a challenge per week, mostly targeting a handful of children's books about LGBTQ+ issues, which at the time was just about all we had. At first, the challenges had quite an edge to them. The library was accused of being part of a larger anti-Christian conspiracy to destroy the family.

I did some public presentations about how the library chose items, and the various aspects of our role as a public institution. In those meetings, I finally found the source of the challenges. At that time, Focus on the Family (FOF, an evangelical ministry operating in Colorado Springs) was pushing a sharply critical message about libraries. They urged young mothers to stay away from the library altogether, lest they or their toddlers be tainted by liberalism. One article in FOF's newsletter, *Citizen,* suggested that the best way to remove books was not to start at the top. Get a page—someone who refiles returned books to the shelf—to misplace something. As detailed in my book *The New Inquisition: Understanding and Managing Library Challenges,* I eventually wound up joining FOF, going so far as to attend their public activism course on how to take over school and library boards and reorient them to a more Christian perspective.

Shortly after, I was bemused to receive a series of personalized and urgent letters from Dr. James Dobson himself, founder and at that time CEO of FOF, ranging from the persecution of Christians in China, to the "great and intolerable sin" of abortion, to the "Gay Agenda" (liberal attempts to turn children into homosexuals), to the appointment of US Supreme Court justices. All the letters ended with the same plea: "Send money."

The next month, FOF launched a political campaign about Christians' latest, most pressing issue—fending off the "Gay Agenda." I can only assume that's the one that generated the biggest response to their previous mailings. Their newsletter no longer mentioned China or abortion. In 1992, in coordination with other religious organizers in the Colorado Springs area, came a proposed statewide constitutional amendment designed to strip away various anti-discrimination measures regarding sexual orientation that had been instituted by the liberal cities of Aspen, Boulder, and Denver. To general astonishment of the citizens, the amendment passed 53 to 47 percent. Following a spurt of counter-activism, it was eventually found unconstitutional by the Supreme Court in 1995.

On the one hand, the concern about gay rights succeeded for a time in mobilizing many people to take political action. Right-wing Christians had surprising political success, at first. On the other hand, the push to eliminate civil liberties for gay people also mobilized those on the left, and ultimately succeeded in securing gay rights more quickly and formally. Of course, today's Supreme Court may revisit the matter.

After careful review of many FOF and legal documents, I honestly don't think such attempted censorship and subsequent political action was a religious issue at all; it was about money. The same thing is true of Critical Race Theory, which is not taught in any elementary school in the country, despite the breathless legislation to protect children from it.

In my own recent taste of the Surge, I wound up corresponding with several people who asserted religious arguments for removing library materials. I acknowledged the right to have deeply held beliefs based on Scripture. The library, however, is a secular institution, based on statute and public policy.

A colleague and friend, a former public library administrator in Fort Wayne, Indiana, once was visited by representatives of Eagle Forum, a conservative, pro-life, religious liberty-focused organization founded by the late Phyliss Schlafly in 1972. The representatives began by asking, "Are you a Christian?"

"I am," my friend replied firmly. "But the library is not."

Cherry-Picking the Verses You Like
One of my challengers quoted a few verses he believed showed that God rejected homosexuality (Genesis 19:1–14). This was accompanied with his rhetorical question about the books he challenged: "Is this [book

that featured a gay sexual relationship] appropriate for children?" My written response said generally that the verses he cited describe an incident in which Lot offers up his virgin daughters for gang rape. Later, he sleeps with them (although the Bible points out that Lot was drunk and it was the daughters' idea). I too asked, "Is that appropriate for children?" My point was that just like challenges to other library materials, one cannot judge the whole book by isolated excerpts. Almost all the tactics used to smear books about LGBTQ+ people could also be used against the Bible. In both cases, the argument is reductive and unfair.

NCOSE, EBSCO, and the Catholic Church

There's an old joke about the guy who goes to a psychiatrist. "I want you to take a look at these ink blots," says the psychiatrist. "What do you see?"

The man looks at the first picture. "A man and a woman making love on a rockslide," he says. "It's pretty torrid."

"Hmm," says the psychiatrist. He shows the man a dozen more pictures. For each one, the man describes a very explicit sexual encounter.

Finally, the psychiatrist says, "I'm afraid I'm going to have to recommend some follow-up counseling. You seem to be utterly obsessed with sex."

"Me?" says the man. "You're the one with all the dirty pictures!"

Many challenges against libraries are often wrapped in "protect the children" rhetoric and come from organizations with strong ties to the Catholic Church. One example is Morality in Media, now rebranded as the National Center on Sexual Exploitation (NCOSE). Several years ago, NCOSE led a national campaign against such magazine content aggregators as EBSCO, the leading provider of research databases and publishing-related content services to libraries and used by millions of students to help do their homework. In my own library, the same fellow who advocated the burning of books frequently touts his membership in the local parish. In April 2023, the Associated Press reported that "More than 150 Catholic priests and others associated with the Archdiocese of Baltimore sexually abused over 600 children and often escaped accountability, according to a long-awaited state report released

Wednesday that revealed the scope of abuse span-
ning 80 years and accused church leaders of decades
of coverups."[10] In May of the previous year, leaders of
the Southern Baptist Convention published a list of
hundreds of ministers and other church workers it
described as being "credibly accused" of sexual abuse.
How many children have been systematically abused
by library leaders, whose exploitation was then cov-
ered up by the ALA? I know of none. In my more
cynical moments, I think religious would-be library
censors attack the library to deflect criticism of their
own faith. If they were serious about protecting children, should they not start in their own house? Or to
cite Matthew 7:3–5: "Why beholdest thou the mote
that is in thy brother's eye, but considerest not the
beam that is in thine own eye?"

Equally ironic has been the long, convoluted, and
even sophisticated search strategies some NCOSE
members use to find what they describe as obscene
content in library databases. The members put a lot
of time into these searches. (Incidentally, teenagers
looking for pornography don't start with library databases; they use Google and their smart phones.) What

the sex-obsessed researchers found wasn't what they said they found. But the notion that "library pushes porn at middle schoolers" gets newspapers to take note, and provides a little PR for the cause.

Religion is a significant part of history, and of the lives of many people. Works on religion belong in libraries, including texts of world faiths. However, their inclusion does not constitute endorsement by the library, nor does any faith have the right to impose their views on those who do not share it, or restrict access to views that may contradict their own.

Anti-Semitism and Misinformation

After the election of Donald Trump in 2016, I received a call from a national newspaper. What did the ALA know about anti-Semitic vandalism in libraries? At the time, we had just one report, back in 2013.

Between Trump's election in November and the end of December, there were exactly eight such acts in American libraries—usually white supremacist graffiti, including swastikas and racial epithets. Clearly, Nazi sympathizers were on the rise in the US. They were also on the rise in Germany, where it was learned that despite strong penalties for promotion of Nazi symbols or speech, many white supremacists had embedded themselves in Germany's police and military. This suggests that banning hate speech doesn't work. It just drives that speech underground, where it's hard to track.

Shortly afterward, I was myself targeted by some Nazi trolls. Their pitch to me was that (a) Amazon's dropping of some pro-Nazi titles constituted censorship and the ALA should do something about it, and (b) if I would just read some key Holocaust denial works (thoughtfully appended), I would see just how reasonable they were.

Of course, Amazon isn't a library. It isn't even a public entity. As a private company, it doesn't have to carry products it doesn't want to, or that it fears would offend the majority of its customers. So it didn't really fall in ALA's wheelhouse.

One must wonder then—why would anyone *want* to stand up for one of the most compelling instances of evil in history? One clue could be found in the ludicrous "fact-finding" of one of their "researchers." A woman called us, demanding to know my "ethnic background." She complained about "disgusting" images of people with dread-locks on the ALA website. She wanted to know if librarians had something against people with pure, Norse lineages? This same woman was later banned on Twitter for hate speech. In other words, the motives were fairly transparent racism.

I found myself thinking afterward about exactly what one is obliged to do when challenged by some-one making wild, outlandish claims. Clearly, not all beliefs, just because they are widely held, are true.

Yet there are some truly loony opinions out there, for instance people who still believe, or profess to believe, that the world is flat. Often, the wilder the beliefs, the more likely the believer is to suffer from logorrhea: excessive and often incoherent wordiness—or the inability to stop writing and writing and writing.

When somebody challenges a library book, the first thing I ask is "Have you read the whole thing?" Is it hypocritical for me to reject the works on Holo-caust denial if I won't even explore their literature?

Here's why I don't think so. First, if I were to spend all my time reading the ravings of madmen, I would never have time for anything else. Second, it isn't necessary. In just an hour or so, I can usually identify and test the claims of extravagant positions.

Let's say you're encountering Holocaust denial for the first time. What are they saying? The three pillars of their argument seem to be:

1. Hitler didn't call for genocide.
2. There were no gas chambers.
3. "Only" a million or so Jews died.

With a brief Google search, you can find the raw footage of Hitler calling for the extermination of the Jews. You can find ample evidence of the existence of gas chambers. Through several demographic methods, it's abundantly clear that more than six million Jews were deliberately exterminated—and not "just" victims of typhus in concentration camps.

The claims of Holocaust deniers are obviously false. You don't have to wade through thousands of websites and spurious documents. Wikipedia or Snopes articles list the source material, and often the refutation has been around for decades. Not only is there no extraordinary proof for extraordinary claims, there's no proof at all, just laziness and lies.

The odd thing to me is that disproving the claims doesn't seem to stop people from repeating them. And that's the best reason I can cite not to spend much time with Holocaust deniers. They are impervious to the evidence. The arguments don't go anywhere.

Intellectual open-mindedness means that sometimes you have to be willing to seriously investigate a surprising opinion. But intellectual integrity does not require you to be held hostage to years of crackpot literature (unless you enjoy that sort of thing). Instead, identify the premises, check out the evidence for them, make up your own mind, and don't get caught up in endless, repetitive recitals of the obvious people who have chosen an invincible ignorance.

Gallup polls record that the importance of religion in one's life is sharply falling in the US, generation by generation. This may be because, to the most diverse generation in our history, religion and conservative politics seem bent on sending messages of exclusion and discrimination, of hate and hypocrisy. This may not be a good strategy for future recruitment.

On the Academy and Safety

When I first became a librarian and spoke about censorship issues with my colleagues, I didn't hear much about censorship in academia. Granted, I still haven't heard about attempts to gut university libraries on the basis of viewpoints (although many libraries have indeed whittled down their collections in the race to go digital). But there have been two disturbing cases.

The first was that of Ward Churchill. A tenured professor at the University of Colorado–Boulder, Dr. Churchill in 2001 wrote an essay entitled, "On the Justice of Roosting Chickens." In it, he asserted that based on various treaty violations and military operations by the United States, we were not entirely blameless for the attacks on 9/11. In short order, the Colorado legislature voted to "shame" Churchill, and thereby "comfort" 9/11 victims. Shaming professors for unpopular positions isn't actually in the legislator's job description; upholding the constitution is. In fact, Churchill was fired from his job. Eventually, he won a court case about it, and $1 in damages. But he didn't get his job back.

A second case happened in my alma mater, the University of Illinois–Urbana. In 2013, Steven Salaita, then a tenured professor at Virginia Tech writing mostly about Indigenous people and Arab-Israel issues, received a job offer from the University of Illinois in Urbana. He accepted the job, and submitted his resignation to Virginia. In 2014, after the job offer, but before the university board met to confirm appointments, some U of I scholars and donors reviewed, and strongly objected to, some of Salaita's posts on Twitter, also made in 2014. The job offer was withdrawn.

While free speech has consequences, and the tone of Salaita's tweets were sometimes less than coolly professional (one of his tweets was, "At this point, if Netanyahu appeared on TV with a necklace made from the teeth of Palestinian children, would anybody be surprised?"), academics might be expected to have passionate feelings about the topic of their studies. Although the case was eventually litigated, and settled for $850,000, the issues remain. As of February 2019, Salaita was unable to find a teaching job in academia. Instead, he was driving a school bus.

Two other areas of academic life highlight less than total acceptance of intellectual freedom. The first is protests. In 2017, many Young Republican clubs at universities fell on the strategy of inviting bad boy speaker Milo Yiannapoulos, a homo- and transphobic Republican who delighted in airing a hodgepodge of extreme right-wing views and generally insulting his audience. The clubs received lots of attention—and landed a lot more gigs for their inflammatory speakers. His 2017 appearance at the University of California–Berkeley, once the home of the student Free Speech Movement, eventually resulted in an estimated $100,000 of property damage, caused by (according to various reports) college students themselves or outside agitators. Yiannapoulos's speech was canceled. For the record: the use of violence to prevent a viewpoint—however childish—from being heard not only doesn't work, but it also elevates the canceled speaker in ways that give them additional attention. There are more focused ways to register disagreement: counter-programming, silent protests, or engaged and thoughtful questions and debate. They may not get quite the same level of media coverage, however. "If it bleeds, it leads" does not ease us into nuanced national conversations.

A second area that has received a fair amount of news coverage and commentary over the past several years is "trigger warnings." At one end, this is nothing more startling than a professor making a brief statement before showing a movie or photographs of something like warfare or rape, that the content may be disturbing or "triggering" to trauma survivors. It's a heads-up. But there's another end to the spectrum, where it seems that anything from eating meat to a lack of politeness is so wrapped up in apologies and warnings that it seems no student has the intestinal fortitude to read an essay about something they hadn't seen and liked before.

While I don't think trigger warnings represent much of a problem for intellectual freedom, they do raise the issue of "safety." Certainly, there are times when one really is physically unsafe—in the middle of a Berkeley riot, for instance. Speech can be used as intimidation, as bullying, as a precursor to violence. But often, "safety" is used to describe an emotional state. One feels disrespected, marginalized, or criticized unfairly. This grievance is then presented as a reason to silence the person who made one feel that way.

Yet, just as the Constitution does not guarantee the right not to be offended, neither does it protect our feelings. I continue to draw a line between speech and action. A citizen (as opposed to an elected official) expressing a viewpoint that I believe is intentionally cruel or abusive—let's use support for the policy of separating immigrant children from their parents as an example—is still just talking. My discomfort with it doesn't entitle me to deny the speaker access to a public space.

Many librarians disagree with me. They believe hate speech, broadly defined, should be "deplatformed" at the library. For instance, hate groups shouldn't be allowed to hold meetings at the library. But that strategy has a predictable outcome: expect the hate group to sue the library on First Amendment grounds. Expect them to win, and maybe exact a settlement. They will still get to hold their meetings at the library. As noted earlier, making neo-Nazi speech illegal in Germany did nothing to eliminate it. It might be better to have these meetings

out in public, so you can see who is attending them, and
what they're saying.

On the Media

I used to believe that only the government could
censor. I thought that citizens acting on their own
couldn't ban a library book, for instance (other
than through theft or property destruction). Censorship takes place when some public entity—the
library, the state legislature, Congress, the Supreme
Court—makes that decision based on the ideas being
expressed. Such censorship may take the form of
suppression, in the sense of forbidding the right to
publish. Child pornography is one example. It is flat-
out illegal to exploit actual children in the making of
photographs or films, certainly a requisite aim. Censorship may happen through onerous restrictions,
fines, penalties, or lawsuits (Florida's "Don't Say Gay"
law, for instance). The First Amendment applies to the
federal government, and to state government through
the Fourteenth Amendment (adopted after the Civil

War, and asserting the authority of the nation over the autonomy of the states).

According to this view, those who demand the silencing of voices they don't agree with are not themselves censors. They're asking the government to be.

But I may be wrong. Sometimes private entities and corporations become powerful enough to take on all the characteristics of a public forum, and to deny access to that platform starts to feel very much like ideological suppression. That's part of the controversy swirling around social media today. Until recently, there really weren't any alternatives to Facebook and Twitter. So if Mark Zuckerberg and Jack Dorsey took a dislike to someone, or that person's views, the CEOs or their designees could kick someone off the platform. The government didn't have anything to say about it. Similarly, it's up to Amazon to decide whether it wants to sell Holocaust-denial books.

Sometimes, of course, the government does step in. Perhaps the new communication media is limited or scarce (think available bandwidths for radio broadcast, hence the creation of the Federal Radio

Commission in 1927). It may also be that the media
has a monopoly—either because it was first and
defined the platform (Facebook and Twitter, again),
or because it was simply more successful in a business
sense (think of the three TV channels that dominated
the air for decades—ABC, CBS, and NBC). Or it may
just be that politicians turn up the heat.

In 1972, the Federal Communications Commission (FCC), a successor to the Federal Radio
Commission, was formed. Its current mission: "The
Federal Communications Commission regulates
interstate and international communications by radio,
television, wire, satellite, and cable in all 50 states, the
District of Columbia and U.S. territories. An indepen-
dent U.S. government agency overseen by Congress,
the Commission is the federal agency responsible
for implementing and enforcing America's communications law and regulations."[11] A centerpiece of the
FCC used to be the so-called Fairness Doctrine (first
established in Federal Radio Commission days). The
Fairness Doctrine stated that "public interest requires
ample play for the free and fair competition of opposing
views, and the Commission believes that the principle

applies to all discussions of issues of importance to the public."[12] The Fairness Doctrine also addressed the idea that if a person was attacked in the media, they had the right to deliver a rebuttal.

The doctrine died, however, in 1987 when the proliferation of channels undercut the notion of scarcity, the Reagan administration seemed opposed to regulation of many kinds, and journalists thought themselves better equipped to determine fair coverage than politicians were. The Supreme Court probably would have slapped it down. Nonetheless, the end of the Fairness Doctrine marked the beginning of the rise of talk radio, and in the end, the "fair and balanced" coverage of Fox News.

In the 1960s, the primetime *Smothers Brothers Show* had many famous fights with "censors"—internal CBS staff who fought to rein in the anti-establishment, politically left-leaning comedy show. Even though this fight over content did reflect political pressures from both the right and left, the actual disputes were contractual, not a matter of constitutional rights.

This highlights another trend: businesses often turn to "self-censorship" in the attempt to avoid governmental regulation. The Comics Code Authority (CCA) was formed in 1954 after a series of Senate hearings and the publication of *Seduction of the Innocent* by psychiatrist Fredric Wertham. Among other things, Wertham claimed that there was a homoerotic undercurrent to Batman and his "ward" Robin. Many comic books added the stamp of the CCA to their covers, although its use was voluntary. Most comics publishers have abandoned it.

In 1968, the Motion Picture Association adopted its film ratings system. Again, the idea was to have its own system of content rating rather than bring down the legislative wrath of government officials. Another factor, no doubt, was to avoid advertiser discomfort.

Similarly, Facebook and Twitter have adopted various advisory groups and internal processes to provide some assurance of whatever "fairness" means these days, although such protocols tend to be far more reactive, volatile, and less tested than statute.

Today, radio, TV, film, and the internet have drifted far from comedian George Carlin's "7 words you can never say." (His 1972 bit named the words then forbidden on TV: "Shit, piss, fuck, cunt, cocksucker, motherfucker, and tits.") Why so little outcry? Because there are now so many programs, stations, and channels, that one can easily find something that perfectly comports with their prejudices. There's no one source that everyone watches.

Still, Facebook postings have been tied to political uprisings around the world (the Arab Spring in Tunisia in 2011, and the January 6 attack on the nation's capital in 2021). Threats of physical violence abound, particularly against women, and particularly on Twitter. Will social media succeed in fending off government regulation, or will the issue fade away with increasing diversification of platforms?

Fake News and the Big Lie

Despite a persistent thread of anti-intellectualism in America, libraries, schools, and universities have until recent times been largely respected. They represent knowledge, the consideration of a body of evidence. Now, however, not only are learning and teaching institutions under attack, but the very idea of truth is also suspect. Now there are "alternative facts," to quote Kellyanne Conway, former senior counselor to ex-President Trump.

In our time, we have seen not just exaggeration for political advantage, but unprecedented and outright lying. The Big Steal—Trump's charge that the 2020 election was "rigged"—is one of them. As with Focus on the Family, the alternative narrative did generate money, and once again, that was probably the point. The many associated lies—voting machines "flipped" votes over the internet, a million dead people voted, China substituted bamboo-based ballots—persisted despite being not only patently absurd, but repeatedly disproven.

I was struck by Trump associate and right-wing architect Steve Bannon's 2018 statement: "The real opposition is the media. And the way to deal with them is to flood the zone with shit."[13] That strategy gave us QAnon, hydroxychloroquine, immigrant caravans "of rapists and murderers and drug dealers," and more.

From a censorship perspective, this is pretty sneaky. It's not about removing books from the library. It's not about challenging assertions with verifiable facts. It's about leaving such a smear of misinformation that it all tends to blur together, so that all that remains is opinion, each as good as another. The effect is the same as an outright ban. It's just more entertaining for some, and people pay for entertainment.

The late twentieth and early twenty-first century have taught us a lot about brain research. The main finding is that we are feeling creatures who think; not thinking creatures who feel. Arguments that "feel right" are often far more persuasive than those that *are* right. This winds up being censorship by distraction. Just keep changing the topic, making up extravagant nonsense and sensationalist claims, and building narratives that identify a villain (see the rise in anti-Semitism and white supremacy, in which Jews and Blacks are "evil"), a victim (e.g., "No one has suffered like we Christians/white people/Republicans have suffered!"), and a hero (whatever authoritarian figure gets on TV the most). Eventually, only the most radical positions make sense, where the echoes are the loudest.

Free Speech to What Purpose?

At this writing, Elon Musk has purchased Twitter for $44 billion and immediately reinstated some highly public personalities previously banned on that platform, including Trump. A self-proclaimed free speech absolutist, Musk assured advertisers that "Twitter obviously cannot become a free-for-all hellscape, where anything can be said with no consequences!"[14] And yet, shortly after his acquisition, use of the N-word on the social media platform promptly rose by almost 500 percent. One consequence has been the defection of advertisers.

Historically, free speech is justified in many ways. It's how we test assumptions to seek the truth (Mill's marketplace of ideas, again). It's how we protest religious or political coercion. It's how we tell the stories of ourselves.

But in our time, it often seems to be the veil for hypocrisy. Why do some people seek absolute freedom in speech? Apparently, they want the untrammeled right to make racist and anti-Semitic slurs. At the same time, they also want to forbid the rights of others to seek information about abortion, or order a birthday cake or website if the businessperson disapproves of the sexual preferences or practices of the customer. They complain about cancel culture, then pass laws banning the discussion of slavery, the genocide of Native Americans, or stories about men who marry men.

There is power in the possession of a platform. But the power to do what? To explore the human story? To find truth or beauty? To lie and misinform in order to achieve even more power?

In 2012, I was contacted by the US State Department to guest lecture in Russia. My library was then experimenting with various ebook business models, and the Russian people are great readers. One of my lectures was to be at a huge book fair in Moscow. I also spoke with a variety of publishers, librarians, academics, and journalists.

When I told my library stories about fairy tales and outrage over vampire sex (the novels of Charlene Harris and the TV series *True Blood*), the Russians were tickled; they found my stories funny. I soon realized that our "censorship" is quite unlike that of what happens in Russia. Earlier in 2012, five members of the feminist band Pussy Riot held an anti-Putin protest performance inside Moscow's Cathedral of Christ the Savior. First, the Orthodox clergy condemned the performance as sacrilegious. Three of the members were arrested for "hooliganism motivated by religious hatred." Two of them were sentenced to two years in prison.

Again, until this latest swing to attack both books and librarians, I can understand why many living in overtly tyrannical societies consider America's censorship problems almost quaint. I fear that in recent years we have taken a distinct step toward Russian-style oligarchy and authoritarianism. What's the tip-off? The merger of religion and state. Neither is particularly open to criticism, and when they have the power to silence and punish apostates, they often take it.

Is that who we want to be?

Will the Censors Win?

Trends aren't straight lines. They're roller coasters and whirligigs. It could be that this recent surge of library challenges is just what it looks like: a callback to 1938, and the precursor to a clash between authoritarianism and democracy. It could be that it's a marginal last gasp of a generation or generations that bitterly protest their own loss of relevance, full of sound and fury, and signifying nothing. It could be the rise of a new, strong, and more dynamic world, more deeply linked, cleansed, and tempered by conflict.

My observation about censorship in our time is this: we get what we deserve. If we defend the freedom to ask questions, the freedom to explore, the freedom to be delighted or confused or challenged, then we continue to grow. This is true both for individuals and for nations. If we narrow our range of possibilities, if we muzzle the voices of people who don't fit the current fashion or faction, then we weaken, become less adaptable or resilient. We stagnate and diminish.

We have a choice.

III.
The Role of the Citizen

Seven Things You Can Do

Faced with malice, deception, growing violence, and undercurrents of tyranny, it's easy to lose heart. But I'd like to end on a happier note. What can you do to build a nation you actually want to live in?

I have seven suggestions.

1. Laugh

In the wonderful book *Being Wrong: Adventures in the Margin of Error*, author Kathryn Schulz notes that toddlers—who fall over when they walk, who can't control their bladders, who get so much wrong—nonetheless laugh, every day, up to a hundred times more often than adults. Maybe they just don't have the ego investment, the sunk costs of many years of fallacious notions. But we have a right to be wrong, and often, it's hilarious. Sometimes, as our comedians demonstrated during the Trump administration, laughter can help us put things in perspective and keep us sane.

2. Talk to your children

I've lost count of the parents who want me to prevent their children from reading, seeing, or hearing something the parents don't approve of. In some cases, they push to require schools or libraries to surveil and report on their children's investigations.

Here's an alternative: stop putting the library or school in the middle and talk to your children directly. What are they looking into? Why do they find it interesting? How do they feel about what they've learned, and how do you feel about their feelings? Few things have so restored my faith in human beings as talking to my own kids. The development of the human mind is a miraculous thing, with many unexpected and even transformative pathways. Why not explore them together?

3. Read more books and talk about them

During the pandemic, I saw a surprising rise of people joining book clubs. Many tackled the issues sweeping the nation—Black Lives Matter protests, for instance. The best book clubs include people and works you wouldn't ordinarily hang out with.

Look around and see what kinds of book clubs already exist in your community, and swing by. The local library is a good place to start.

I also recommend *family* book clubs. I mentioned the importance of talking to your children. Why not read with them, too? If you think some current young adult title your son or daughter wants to read is just too out there for you to be comfortable with, then read it with them, and talk about what you did and didn't like about it. Then recommend a title you think is more "appropriate." Read that with your children too, and see what *they* think of it. Usually, our children start out kind of sharing the values we taught them. But testing those values is part of becoming an adult.

Be prepared to learn how the world has changed since your childhood, and just how insightful your child may be.

4. Support the newspapers

During the period in which many midwestern libraries were established (roughly 1870–1930), community leaders justified the founding of libraries by emphasizing the importance of "well-informed citizens." If we want to build nations we actually want to live in, we need to know what's happening. What are the issues of the day, both urgent and emerging? What's real and what's speculation? So I think it is incumbent on Americans to subscribe to and read at least one reputable national newspaper.

I worry about local papers. The business model for journalism used to be based on advertising. Now much of that advertising has moved to the internet. Across the nation, journalist staffing has fallen precipitously, and many smaller newspapers have shut down. This means there's no one to monitor town council meetings, county planning committees, school board sessions, or library board discussions.

So it's vital to support not just the national news, but what may remain of your local newspaper.

Whether your bias is business or government, we all need to be watched. Most people are ethical. The ones that aren't can do a lot of damage. We need fearless journalism as much as we need fearless librarianship.

Contribute to the paper, too. I was a newspaper columnist for twenty-five years, and one of the things I learned was that it is a very small percentage of the public that writes a letter to the editor. Silence is often taken as assent. People in a community may feel that they are far out of step with a prevailing sentiment. But that's just because a handful of loud voices are taking up all the air. As Eric Hoffer put it, revolutions begin with "men of militant words." Only later are there "men of action." Weigh in on the things that matter to you. You may be surprised to discover that many people agree with you, and are just waiting for someone brave enough to step up and begin to articulate other courses of action.

5. Volunteer

There has been a great deal of research about what leads to happiness. It turns out that one of the best strategies—way better than making a lot of money—is helping others. Whether you're still in the workaday world or retired, volunteering with some cause that interests you has multiple outcomes. It helps you build a network of human connection. It helps you improve your local environment. It gets you out of your own head. It builds community. It helps blunt censorship at the core by establishing common ground and shared concerns.

6. Attend civic meetings

Usually, the public only shows up to public meetings when they're mad about something. That often leads to rudeness, incivility, and angry division. Here's an alternative: show up to city, county, school, and library meetings. Even check out the state legislature. Pay attention to the players and the issues. Ask polite questions. Thank them for their service. It can be hard to feel like you're making a difference about national or global issues. But you can make a difference in your community. And many of the folks who work in local government put in long hours. They deserve our thanks.

7. Speak up

Finally, speak up. Nobody enjoys being yelled at. But I have learned, despite the occasional tussle over free speech, that most human beings do have that deep thirst for meaningful conversation.

It may be a bit of a risk to utter what you fear may be an unpopular opinion. But you can't delegate your conscience to others. And we can't learn and grow if we don't step outside of the sandbox. We can't prepare for a future if we can't move beyond the past.

Another kind of speaking up is voting. The fewer hands that hold the reins of power, the greater the likelihood of oppression and suppression. Register to vote, follow the issues, and show up on election day to cast your vote. Our nation, our world, depends on our thoughtful participation and principled action.

***

> *"For every complex problem there is an answer that is clear, simple, and wrong."*
>
> —H. L. Mencken

What could be simpler than telling people you believe to be wrong that they should just shut up? The problem, of course, is that you might be wrong yourself. Or even if the other people *are* wrong, they are on their own journeys of discovery. Being wrong is one of the ways we learn. And if we only have the freedom to agree with each other, we have no freedom at all.

And of course, in a nation where the First Amendment is deeply embedded in our laws and psyches, we don't actually have the right to go around shushing everyone who disagrees with us. There is an expressive quality to speech, beyond its truth-seeking.

Yet every time is different, even when the issues feel very familiar. What can we learn from our time?

First, it's clear that the rise of authoritarianism around the world is picking up steam. One of its markers is the attempted censorship of journalists, teachers, writers, and artists. Today's Republican Party, with its heavy-handed application of laws banning certain ideas and speech (information about abortion, textbooks focusing on race relations, or works reflecting the spectrum of human sexuality) can no longer claim to be the party of free speech.

Second, the emerging political and sociological makeup of America is changing. In the decades to come, the US will be less white, more diverse, and likely more conscious of historic and systemic racism. The minority is becoming the majority, and that may inflame long resentments on both sides. (It's easy to see why oppressed minorities would be resentful. It's less obvious but no less true that the oppressors too are resentful—especially when they get caught.)

Third, the internet, with its anonymity and accidental extremism (algorithms that move people into ever more radical conversational cohorts), has proved to be a profoundly destabilizing influence. Behavior that once would have been utterly unacceptable and acknowledged as false is now monetized, seen as both entertaining and profitable. As with many reality shows, the reality doesn't matter.

Capable and self-confident people are not threatened by speech, nor cowed by unfamiliar viewpoints. They find the world full of potential and wonder. They also find it complex and sometimes dangerous—circumstances that are best addressed through thoughtful exploration and discussion. To fight censorship is to fight fear and ignorance.

We may take some comfort in the fact that ultimately, censorship is also ineffective. When digital information can be shared instantaneously and globally, the attempt to suppress an idea is doomed. Rather, we need to develop the skills to think critically, to consider the source, to examine the evidence, to weigh its effects, and to contribute to the human conversation with compassion, care, and insight. We learn by thinking, not by denying thought.

If censorship is fear, then its opposite is courage. Let us face the world as it is and build a better one.

Notes

1. James LaRue, "*Uncle Bobby's Wedding*," *MyLibBlog*, July 14, 2008, http://jaslarue.blogspot.com/2008/07/uncle-bobbys-wedding.html, accessed May 2, 2023.

2. "What's Behind the Recent Surge in Book Censorship Efforts?" February 1, 2022, Darik.News/USA, https://darik.news/usa/usa/whats-behind-the-recent-surge-in-book-censorship-efforts.html, accessed May 2, 2023.

3. Letter from Matt Krause to Texas Education, October 25, 2021, cited in https://static.texastribune.org/media/files/965725d7f01b8a25ca44b6fde2f5519b/krauseletter.pdf?_ga=2.268317262.1138840670.1640887720-1019961885.1638287134, accessed May 1, 2023.

4. "Standridge Files Bills to Address Indoctrination in Oklahoma Schools," December 16, 2021, https://oksenate.gov/press-releases/standridge-files-bills-address-indoctrination-oklahoma-schools, accessed May 1, 2023.

5. "New ALA Poll Shows Voters Oppose Book Bans: Majority of Survey Respondents Support Librarians and Oppose Banning Books from Public and School Libraries," *American Libraries*, March 24, 2022, https://americanlibrariesmagazine.org/blogs/the-scoop/new-ala-poll-shows-voters-oppose-book-bans/, accessed May 1, 2023.

6. *ALA Bulletin* 33, no. 11 (October 15, 1939).

7. Eric Hoffer, *The True Believer: Thoughts on the Nature of Mass Movements* (HarperCollins e-books, 2011), 26.

8. Ibid., 79.

9. Ibid., 130.

10. Lea Skene, Brian Witte, and Sarah Brumfield, "Report Details 'Staggering' Church Sex Abuse in Maryland," AP News, April 5, 2023, https://apnews.com/article/baltimore-archdiocese-sex-abuse-report-7d5d3af098da59a1c9313a246566638c, accessed May 1, 2023.

11. Federal Communications Commission (FCC), BroadbandUSA, https://broadbandusa.ntia.doc.gov/resources/federal/federal-permitting/federal-communications-commission-fcc, accessed May 1, 2023.

12. Audrey Perry. "Fairness Doctrine," The First Amendment Encyclopedia, updated May 2017 by John R. Vile, https://www.mtsu.edu/first-amendment/article/955/fairness-doctrine, accessed May 1, 2023.

13. Michelle Ye Hee Lee, "Donald Trump's False Comments Connecting Mexican Immigrants and Crime," *Washington Post*, July 8, 2015, https://www.washingtonpost.com/news/fact-checker/wp/2015/07/08/donald-trumps-false-comments-connecting-mexican-immigrants-and-crime/, accessed May 1, 2023.

14. Levin, Tim. "Elon Musk Says 'Twitter Obviously Cannot Become a Free-for-All Hellscape' without Consequences in Bid to Calm Advertisers," Business Insider, October 27, 2022, https://www.businessinsider.com/elon-musk-tells-advertisers-twitter-will-have-free-speech-limits-2022-10, accessed May 1, 2023.

Bibliography

Brannen, Sarah S. *Uncle Bobby's Wedding*. New York: G. P. Putnam's Sons Books for Young Readers, 2008.

Crenshaw, Kimberlé. *Critical Race Theory*. New York: The New Press, 1995.

Finan, Christopher M. *How Free Speech Saved Democracy: The Untold History of How the First Amendment Became an Essential Tool for Securing Liberty and Social Justice*. Truth to Power, 2022.

Garnar, Martin, and Trina J. Magi. *Intellectual Freedom Manual*. Chicago: ALA Editions, 2021.

Haight, Jonathan. *The Righteous Mind: Why People Are Divided by Politics and Religion*. New York: Vintage Books, 2013.

Hentoff, Nat. *Free Speech for Me—But Not for Thee: How the American Left and Right Relentlessly Censor Each Other*. New York: HarperCollins, 1992.

Hoffer, Eric. *The True Believer: Thoughts on the Nature of Mass Movements*. New York: Harper Perennial Modern Classics, 2002.

Lakoff, George. *The ALL NEW Don't Think of an Elephant! Know Your Values and Frame the Debate*. White River Junction, VT: Chelsea Green Publishing, 2014.

LaRue, James. *The New Inquisition: Understanding and Managing Intellectual Freedom Challenges.* Westport, CT: Libraries Unlimited, 2007.

Lipstadt, Deborah. *Denying the Holocaust: The Growing Assault on Truth and Memory.* New York: Plume, 1994.

Mills, John Stuart. *On Liberty.* New York: Liberal Arts Press, 1956.

Nye, Valerie, and Kathy Barco. *True Stories of Censorship Battles in America's Libraries.* Chicago: American Library Association, 2012.

Oldmann, Shannon M. *The Fights Against Book Bans: Perspectives from the Field.* Santa Barbara, CA: ABC CLIO, 2023.

Snyder, Timothy. *On Tyranny: Twenty Lessons from the Twentieth Century.* New York: Tim Duggan Books, 2017.

Strauss, William, and Neil Howe. *Generations: the History of America's Future, 1584 to 2069.* New York: Morrow, 1991.